THE WORLD'S
GREATEST
MYSTERIES

THE WORLD'S
GREATEST
MYSTERIES

JOYCE ROBINS

FOREWORD BY COLIN WILSON

GALLERY BOOKS
An Imprint of W. H. Smith Publishers Inc.
112 Madison Avenue
New York City 10016

First published in Great Britain in 1989 by
The Octopus Publishing Group

This edition published in 1989 by Gallery Books
an imprint of W. H. Smith Publishers Inc.
112 Madison Avenue,
New York City 10016

© 1989 Octopus Books Ltd

ISBN 083179 674 X

Produced by Mandarin Offset
Printed and Bound in Hong Kong

CONTENTS

Foreword by Colin Wilson

As a lifelong collector of Unsolved Mysteries, I have to pay a respectful tribute to the compiler of this volume; there is not a single important case that he missed. But the book is more than just a collection of oddities. As I read through it, I realised that it is also a kind of jigsaw puzzle, in which many of the interlocking parts are scattered in different parts of the book. The attentive reader who recognises the connections may begin to see the emergence of a strange and fascinating pattern.

Let me describe my own experience as an investigator of the unsolved. In the late 1960s, when the 'occult revival' had been in full swing for almost a decade, I was asked by an American publisher if I would be interested in writing a book about 'the occult.' I agreed because it seemed an interesting challenge, and because, like most people, I had always been fascinated by mysteries like Atlantis, the poltergeist, the Loch Ness monster, the curse of Tutankhamen, and so on. But I also had a strong suspicion that, on closer examination, most of them would turn out to be laughable absurdities. In fact, as I began to research *The Occult*, I became increasingly impressed by the consistency of the evidence. There could be no doubt whatever that thousands of normal, well-balanced individuals had experienced baffling encounters with 'the occult.'

Consider, for example, the following case. In May 1863, Charles Dickens dreamed that a lady in a red shawl was standing in front of him. He assumed it was someone he knew, but when she turned round he saw it was a stranger, who introduced herself as Miss Napier. As he was dressing the next morning he thought how absurd it was to have a dream about a non-existent stranger. That evening he gave one of his famous readings, and while he was relaxing in his dressing room afterwards, two friends came to see him, accompanied by a woman he instantly recognised as the lady in the red shawl. She was introduced to him as Miss Napier...

It sounds a curious but not particularly weird coincidence – until you begin to think about its implications. If Dickens is correct when he insists that he had never heard of Miss Napier before his dream, then he somehow dreamed of the future. And that implies, at the very least, that this ordinary, solid world that surrounds us is the facade of a far more complex and mysterious reality, in which – in some sense – everything that is going to happen has already taken place. As I read this story – in Dickens' own account – I seemed to see that solid facade shimmering, and becoming for a moment transparent. And again and again, as I wrote *The Occult*, I experienced this disturbing but exciting sensation.

Yet my approach to these 'mysteries' remained basically scientific. The answer, it seemed to me, was simply that *all* human beings possess 'hidden powers' of which they are normally unaware. Is there anyone who has not thought about some friend or relative he hasn't heard of in years, then received a letter from him in the next morning's post? Or experienced curious flashes of telepathy in which he knew what someone was about to say? Or come across some unusual word or fact for the first time, then heard it several times more in the next few days? The psychical

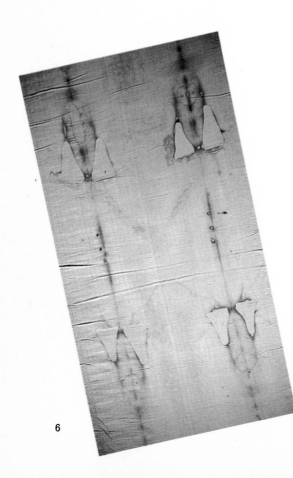

investigator Nandor Fodor, who was also a Freudian psychiatrist, was convinced that the answer lay in the powers of the unconscious mind. It was Fodor who first suggested, for example, that the incredible behaviour of the poltergeist, or 'banging ghost', is due to the unconscious mind of some disturbed child or adolescent, a theory which is now generally accepted.

I myself found this theory highly satisfying – even though it fails to explain *how* someone's unconscious mind can cause objects to fly around the room – until I started to research a book on the poltergeist, and studied hundreds of cases, some at first hand. And then, to my dismay, I came to a highly disturbing conclusion. There have been cases in which poltergeist manifestations have taken place in *empty* houses, or continued in the same house when there have been a whole series of tenants. That obviously suggested that the poltergeist was an *independent* entity, which merely 'borrowed' energy from the disturbed children. This conclusion was supported by another investigator, Guy Playfair, who had investigated many 'poltergeist hauntings' in Brazil, and had come to the conclusion that many of them were *caused* by a specialist in *umbanda* (the Brazilian form of voodoo) who could somehow bribe or persuade the poltergeist to make a nuisance of itself. Half a century earlier, another investigator, Max Freedom Long, concluded that the *kahunas*, or magician priests of Hawaii, have the power to cause death by the 'death prayer', which again involves making use of a 'poltergeist.' (This present book begins by citing a number of similar cases.)

All this, I agree, will strike most readers as unutterably wild and absurd. I can only say that, after twenty years of study, I have reached the reluctant conclusion that these are not superstitious delusions, but that they are firmly based on fact. I do not advise people to spend too much time brooding on the existence of 'spirits' – for it seems to be a kind of rule of the psychic realm that if you ignore them they will usually ignore you – but I believe that a recognition of their existence is an important step in catching a glimpse behind that shimmering facade that separates us from the realm of a wider reality.

Of course, there are many lesser mysteries to which I think I have found the solution. In the case of the *Mary Celeste*, for example, it has been discovered that the cover had been blown off the hold, and that the hold was full of barrels of industrial alcohol. Almost certainly what happened was that a single barrel blew its top, and the captain, afraid that the whole ship might blow up, ordered the crew to take to the boats – as a temporary measure – but forgot to secure the boats to the ship with a line. Then a wind blew up suddenly, the *Mary Celeste* receded into the distance, leaving them all to die at sea. As to the Bermuda Triangle, much reliable evidence indicates that the problem there is a 'magnetic vortex' – of the kind which causes birds to lose their way over certain areas of the earth – which is probably triggered at intervals by movements in the earth's core. The problem of the Man in the Iron Mask obviously hinges upon the fact that the king was anxious *that his face should not be seen*, which suggests that he bore a strong resemblance to the king, and was therefore some relative – perhaps a bastard brother – who knew some dangerous royal secret. To these, and to many other problems, I can suggest solutions. But to the mystery implied in the story about Charles Dickens, and in many other cases in this book, the only solution is to recognise that mankind will need to achieve a new level of evolutionary consciousness before they can be understood.

CHAPTER ONE

THE
POWER
OF THE
MIND

◆

The depth and complexity of the human mind is still one of the world's greatest mysteries and we have hardly begun to probe its capabilities. Belief that some people could glimpse the future or kill an enemy through a curse seems as old as history itself, but far more recent are claims that the mind can cause metal objects to bend or that, under hypnosis, we can go back into past lives. All the techniques of science make little headway when attempting to probe the powers of the mind but, however much research is undertaken, we can be sure there will be a great deal more to discover.

Curses and Maledictions

TRADITIONS OF SORCERY THROUGHOUT THE WORLD

Anthropologists have always recognized the power of the curse in primitive religions. In many tribes the very act of cursing was enough to kill a man; African witch-doctors obtained power over their victims by collecting their hair and nail clippings; Australian aborigines would ritually 'point the bone'.

Ronald Rose, an anthropologist who made a study of aboriginal customs, cited the case of a man who had raped two young girls being 'boned' by a wise man of the tribe. The old man hammered a point on to the end of a piece of wire, then made a fire and, as he recited his curses, drew his 'bone' backwards and forwards across the flames and then pointed it in the wrongdoer's direction. He did this every night for a week, during which time the victim took to his bed, growing weaker until, on the last night of the ritual, he died.

Rose's story is only one of many eye-witness accounts of witchcraft and voodoo killings in lands where tribal magic is traditionally part of a way of life; over the past 50 years or so, however, there have been reports of similar deaths in a number of American cities.

Death by the Hex

Doctors in the USA called one puzzling phenomenon the 'Oriental nightmare death syndrome'. In 1951 a Honolulu pathologist reported performing post-mortems on 85 Filipino men who had died suddenly after the onset of violent nightmares. No natural cause of death was found in a single case but the men's families had no doubt that their deaths were due to curses. The Filipino name for the illness was simply *bangungut*, or 'nightmare' and, once afflicted, no one was expected to recover.

Above: *Voodoo dancers, supposedly possessed by gods, go into a trance.* **Right:** *Summoning up the spirits.*

Above: *Burning an effigy of the person accursed.*

Voodoo

Professor M. Golden, who as a doctor has a practice in the Deep South of the USA, has reported on cases of voodoo death in the *American Journal of Psychiatry* and has no doubt that he has seen more than a dozen cases of the hex in operation. Among his patients was a 33-year-old man, hexed by his mistress who was well-known for her powers; he exhibited all the signs of severe neurological illness and, though all the tests proved normal, died within a fortnight. Another man had been hexed by his wife who suspected him of being unfaithful; two previous husbands had already died from unidentified illnesses.

Modern psychologists admit that mental attitudes can have a powerful effect on physical well-being and favour the theory that curses can only kill through the strong belief of the victim. Sandford Cohen, a psychologist from Boston University in the United States, says the key lies in the feelings of utter helplessness and hopelessness engendered by a curse. Most doctors agree that it is fear that kills, rather than any magical power of the hex; one reaction to extreme fear seems to be that the heart-beat slows and blood pressure drops, to the extent that death might eventually result, or it could be that the lungs become paralyzed so that they no longer pump the vital oxygen around the body.

In 1966 doctors in Baltimore City Hospital recorded a case of a black woman patient who grew weaker before their eyes, even though her vital organs were all healthy and there seemed to be no medical reason for her condition. She had been one of triplets born in the swamplands of Georgia where a midwife had told her mother that the babies were hexed: the first would die before she was 16, the second before she was 21 and the third before she was 23. The first sister was killed in a car accident at the age of 15 and the second was the victim of an accidental shooting on her 21st birthday. The patient was the third girl in the ill-fated family. After a day when she had exhibited all the signs of extreme panic, she died on the eve of her twenty-third birthday, in spite of all the doctors' efforts. No medical condition showed up in the post mortem.

Though many hexes fit this psychological explanation, there are other well-attested examples of victims being badly affected by curses they know nothing about and would certainly not have believed in. In the 1950s a photographer, Hassold Davis, attending the coronation of King Essey Bonzon in West Africa, woke to find himself paralyzed down one side, just as though a line had been drawn down his body from the middle of his forehead. The pain was severe but when he called the mission doctor he was told that no medical treatment could help. The symptoms were the result of a well-known local spell. He reluctantly consulted one of the king's sorcerers who removed the curse, and the pain and paralysis disappeared immediately.

Witchcraft in Britain

In Britain, the traditions of sorcery have always been linked to witchcraft rather than voodoo. In past centuries there was a tendency to ascribe any disaster, from the failure of crops to the death of a child, to the 'evil eye' of a neighbourhood witch, and many old women guilty of nothing more than brewing up a few home-made herbal remedies were persecuted as witches.

Left: A traditional witch poppet used to kill or torture someone. The poppet would have nails or thorns driven through its body. Below: A woodcut showing the devil instructing witches in the art of making waxen images.

A Witch's Curse

A real witch's curse was probably just as effective as that of a voodoo priest or an African *ju-ju* man. One of the Abingdon witches executed in 1579, Mother Dutton, was accused of murdering four people by sticking thorns in the sides of images, while John Palmer and Elizabeth Knott, executed in St Albans in 1647, were said to have fashioned a clay doll and burned it, causing their victim to suffer terrible agonies before death.

In 1613 the 11 witches of Pendle, in Lancashire, went on trial for a total of 16 murders. One of the accused, 80-year-old Elizabeth Southerns, admitted that the favourite method of disposing of an enemy was to make a doll in his or her image, then piercing it with a thorn or a pin. Elizabeth Southerns died in prison but the other 10 witches were convicted and hanged.

One of the witches, old Chattox, is said to have left a legacy of evil behind her. When one of the farmers of Pendle ordered her off his hand she urinated on the spot, telling him that it was cursed and that he would never graze his cattle there again. Local people still remember cattle dying in that particular field, then, in the 1950s, inspectors from the Ministry of Agriculture reported that the trouble was due to an unusual poisonous weed. Modern technology disposed of the problem but no one has ever been able to explain why the weed grew in that field and no other.

Though it might be comforting to think of the witch's curse as belonging to a primitive era long ago, curse dolls, with nails or thorns driven through their bodies, have been found more than once in rural areas over the past 20 years. In 1947 the *News Chronicle* reported that a man who attacked an old woman explained that she had been torturing him through curses for five years. She claimed that she had only been gathering parsley on his land, while he was convinced that she was preparing a new hex at the time.

The Power of the Curse

Dismissing curses as no more than mumbo-jumbo may be dangerous but equally it may be only too tempting to manufacture or imagine them. When the Sunshine Skyway Bridge, at Tampa Bay in Florida, seemed to have a jinx on it after 60 people died in four separate shipping disasters, local fishermen came up with the story that a construction worker had put a curse on it. He was supposed to have fallen into wet concrete and to be there still, as part of the cursed structure.

In 1972 two small stone heads were dug up from the back garden of a house in Hexham, Northumberland. No sooner were they taken into the house than all sorts of weird poltergeist phenomena began to afflict the family. There were sightings of a terrifying half-man, half-beast, who apparently followed the heads when they were sent to a folklore expert in Southampton. Stories of an ancient Celtic curse soon took hold, but a previous occupant of the house, Desmond Craigie, explained that he had carved the heads for his daughter, 15 years before. Later tests showed that the heads were artificially moulded, not carved from natural stone.

Left: A reminder that witchcraft exists today. Two effigies and a sheep's heart which mysteriously appeared at Castle Rising, Yorkshire, at the waning of the moon. Above: Ruins of North Berwick church, regularly used to celebrate the witch's sabbath.

The Curse of Tutankhamen

THE CURSE OF THE PHARAOH

The tradition of curses on those who dare to plunder a tomb goes back to the very beginnings of Egyptian history, for the ancient Egyptians believed that such desecration would make the spirit homeless. The curse formulae found in tombs threaten punishment and death to grave-robbers; one threatens that the Nekhebet bird shall scratch the face of anyone violating a tomb.

The Legacy of Tutankhamen
One of the most enduring curses seems to be the one attached to the tomb of the boy king Tutankhamen. When the English archaeologist Lord Carnarvon and his American partner Howard Carter entered the Pharaoh's tomb in the Valley of the Kings at Luxor in 1922 they found it packed with priceless treasures. They also found a tablet with a curse written in

hieroglyphics: 'Death will slay with his wings whoever disturbs the pharaoh's peace.'

Two months after his entry into the tomb, 56-year-old Lord Carnarvon was dead. He had been suffering from a violent fever and in his delirium he murmured over and over again: 'A bird is scratching my face.' At the exact moment of his death all the lights in Cairo went out, then came on again five minutes later.

Carnarvon's death was only the first. American millionaire George Jay-Gould, a friend of Carnarvon, died from a fever soon after visiting the tomb. British industrialist Joel Woolf, one of the first visitors to view the tomb, fell into a coma and died on the boat home to England.

By 1929, 22 people who had been involved with Tutankhamen's tomb had died prematurely; 13 of these had been present at its discovery. Within seven years only two of the original excavators were still alive.

The curse of the pharaohs has continued to follow the Tutankhamen treasures. In 1966 when the Egyptian director of antiquities was asked to arrange an exhibition in Paris, he dreamed that he would be in danger if the Pharaoh's treasures left Egypt. As he left a meeting called to discuss detailed arrangements, he was knocked down by a car and killed.

His successor, Dr Gamal Mehrez, pointed out that he had been involved with tombs and mummies all his life yet he was still healthy, so he was living proof that all the tragedies had been pure coincidence. In 1972, however, as the gold mask of Tutankhamen left the museum for its air journey to London, he fell dead.

Howard Carter, joint leader of the expedition, always refused to believe in any sort of curse and no mysterious fate overtook him; he died of natural causes in 1939. If the curse of the tomb works in the same way as voodoo curses, by working on the mind of the victim, his sturdy disbelief could be the key to his survival.

Death in the Tombs

Journalist Philipp Vandenburg, who studied the legend of the Pharaoh's curse, argues that a people capable of building marvels like the pyramids would not have abandoned their kings to the mercy of robbers without finding some way of protecting them, and that the ancient Egyptians were masters in the art of poison. Some lethal poisons work through contact and, if used in wall paintings or the trappings of the tomb,

might have remained effective for thousands of years in the hermetically sealed environment.

In 1949 atomic scientist Professor Louis Bulgarini came up with the theory that the ancient Egyptians might have covered the floor of the tombs with uranium, or finished the graves with radio-active rock.

A more prosaic explanation might be some form of bacteria, flourishing in the enclosed atmosphere and passing on infection to some of the visitors but not others. Later deaths, through car accidents or heart attack, would have been mere coincidences. Dr Ezzedin Taha, a Cairo biologist who put forward this idea at a news conference in 1962, was killed in a car crash shortly afterwards.

Once the legend of a curse takes hold it feeds on such coincidences but many people still believe that when modern archaeologists rifle the tombs, violating the sacred beliefs of those buried there, they must expect to pay for their actions.

Left: When a team of archaeologists broke into the tomb of Tutankhamen they found his mummified body inside a gold coffin. *Above:* The solid gold death mask of the boy king was one of the many treasures discovered in the tomb.

Hypnosis

THE POWER OF THE UNCONSCIOUS

In the 18th century when Franz Mesmer developed his technique of 'animal magnetism', claiming to cure asthma, paralysis and a wide variety of other complaints that did not respond to conventional methods of treatment, he was denounced as a charlatan.

The medical establishment of the day ridiculed his theory that illness results from the inbalance of a magnetic fluid that fills the universe and that the magnetism he practised could restore its natural flow and bring the patient back to health. But some doctors in France and England went on to experiment for themselves and discovered that a subject in a mesmeric trance could be convinced that he experienced no pain, even when under normal circumstances he would have been screaming.

A Scottish surgeon, working in India, performed pain-free amputations as well as thousands of minor operations and the Indian government was so impressed that he was put in charge of a hospital named the Mesmeric Hospital.

It soon became obvious that no mystic fluids were involved and that the trance itself was no magic cure, only a way of helping a patient to concentrate on what he was told. It became known as hypnotism, from the Greek word *hypnos*, meaning sleep.

Hypnotism made such excellent theatrical entertainment, with stage hypnotists delighting audiences by telling their subjects to bark like dogs or jump like kangaroos, that most doctors were reluctant to use it. As an anaesthetic it was quickly overshadowed by ether and chloroform, which did not bring with them the same aura of suspicion.

Hypnosis as an Aid to Medicine

In France, a handful of doctors persevered with hypnotism, finding that suggestions given to hypnotised patients could be an effective healing tool.

It was Sigmund Freud who saw the possibilities for psychotherapy and began using hypnotism to take patients back through their lives to unearth traumatic events long hidden in the unconscious mind. He found that, as a first step to curing a neurosis, it was important to unearth and understand these long-forgotten experiences.

More recently, hypnosis has been used

Below: Franz Mesmer's 'Magic Tub', a piece of equipment he used in curing ailments which had failed to respond to conventional treatment. The word 'mesmerize' was taken from Mesmer's name. Subjects in 'mesmeric' trances were convinced they experienced no pain, though if they had been properly conscious they would have been screaming.

to cure allergies, insomnia and addictions such as smoking or over-eating. American dentists have found that its use can make for not only painless extractions but faster healing afterwards.

In 1952 the *British Medical Journal* reported the amazing case of a 16-year-old boy who had been cured of congenital ichthyosis, in which a warty layer covered most of his body. It often cracked, leading to infection, and smelled so bad that he was unable to go to school or mix normally with other people.

Plastic surgeons at East Grinstead tried grafting some of the unaffected skin from his chest on to his hand but within a few weeks the new skin had developed a horny layer. As a last resort he was hypnotized, the hypnotist telling him that the condition would disappear from his left arm. Within 10 days the warty layer had softened and fallen off, leaving the whole arm clear. More sessions of hypnosis followed, clearing one area after another, until the boy was able to return to normal life.

Regression into Past Lives

Over the past 40 years, arguments over hypnosis have centred on claims that subjects can regress not only to their childhood but also into past lives.

In the early 1950s an amateur American hypnotist from Colorado was taking a 29-year-old Wisconsin housewife, Virginia Tighe, back to her childhood through hypnotic regression when she began talking as Bridey Murphy, saying that she was born in Cork, Ireland, on 20 December 1798. In an Irish accent she described her life in minute detail; she was the daughter of a Protestant barrister, living in a secluded house outside Cork and at 17 married Brian Joseph McCarthy, then moved to Belfast and lived in a house in Dooley Road. Bridey died at 66 after falling downstairs and breaking her hip and Mrs Tighe was able to describe her funeral and tombstone.

Bernstein's book *The Search for Bridey Murphy* brought hypnotic regression to wide public attention and newspaper investigators were able to find distant relatives of Irish extraction who might have provided Virginia Tighe with some information on life in Ireland but no one ever managed to provide a complete explanation of what had happened.

She had accurately described a journey from Belfast to Cork, mentioned shopping at a family firm of grocers called Farr and Carrigan, which had existed at the time, and had used authentic words like 'ditching' for burying and 'linen' for

handkerchief. An 1801 map of Cork showed an area called The Meadows with a ring of houses round it, just as Bridey described it.

Critics made a great deal of the fact that she talked about a metal bed though such a thing was, they said, unknown in Ireland before 1850. Further investigation, however, unearthed advertisements for metal beds as early as 1802.

Thousands of people have apparently re-lived former lives through hypnotic regression, many of them giving facts corroborated by later research. One of the best known was Hollywood actor Glen Ford, who was hypnotized by a doctor in 1978 when he was 61. In the first session, Ford spoke emotionally about being ambushed and shot in a previous existence as Charlie Bill, a Colorado cowboy who worked for a rancher called Charlie Goodnight. Researchers from the University of California, in Los Angeles, went to Colorado to investigate and found that both Bill and Goodnight had lived there, at the time indicated.

Above: *A French eighteenth-century caricature of Mesmer depicting him as a donkey using a technique of animal magnetism. The French medical establishment of the time ridiculed Mesmer's claim that illness resulted from an imbalance of a magnetic fluid that fills the universe and that the magnetism he practised could restore its natural flow and brings patients back to health.*

Glen Ford

The second tape-recorded session took place at the university and this time Ford spoke of life as Charles Stuart from Elgin, Scotland, a piano teacher who described his pupils as 'young flibbertigibbets', a dated expression for frivolous children. Ford even played the piano under hypnosis, though he later admitted that ordinarily he could not play a note. Then researchers who travelled to Elgin discovered the grave of Charles Stuart, who died in 1840.

'That shook me real bad,' said Ford, who had been reluctant to accept the evidence of the tapes as proof of reincarnation as it conflicted with his religious beliefs. I felt immediately that it was the place where I was buried.'

Some Case Histories

There are many more extraordinary cases like these. Beverly Richardson of Northridge, California, regressed in front of TV cameras, talking as Mrs Jean Macdonald, 40 years old in 1898, living in a small Ohio town called Corning. None of the Richardson family had ever visited Corning, yet she was able to describe the town as the older residents remembered it and correctly identify pictures of places in Corning, picking out the changes made since Jean Macdonald's time.

An Indianapolis housewife, Mrs Norbert Williams, talked vividly over several successive sessions as a Confederate soldier, Jean Donaldson from Louisiana. She gave detailed information on civil war battles – Donaldson lost an eye in one and was killed in another, two years later – and mentioned a neighbour, James Duncan, and a friend, Walter Street. Later investigations showed that a Jean Donaldson had lived at a farm near Shreveport in Louisiana and joined the Confederate army in 1862. Both Duncan and Street were also Shreveport residents at the time.

Jane Evans

Welsh hypnotist Arnall Bloxham worked with several hundred subjects, producing remarkable results, particularly in the case of Jane Evans who regressed to six different 'lives'. As Livonia, in AD 286, she was the wife of Titus, tutor in Latin and Greek to Constantine, later the Emperor of Rome. Professor Brian Hartley of Leeds University, an expert on Roman Britain, found that the majority of names and historical facts that she produced were correct, though many were quite obscure, and likely to be known only to historians.

In a later 'life' Jane Evans became Rebecca, a Jewess living in 12th century York, who was massacred along with other Jews in a church crypt. The church was easily identifiable from her descriptions as St Mary's, Cripplegate but, as it had no crypt, the story seemed in doubt. It was only months later, when workmen were carrying out repairs, that they discovered St Mary's lost crypt, just as Rebecca had described it.

Another of Bloxham's subjects was Graham Huxtable, whose soft Welsh lilt became a strong south of England accent as he recounted his experiences as an illiterate gunner's mate in the war at sea between England and France at the turn of the 18th century. His out-of-date shipboard slang and the archaic naval practices he described were all verified by experts at the National Maritime Museum at Greenwich.

Above: The hypnotist has all his 'subjects' under total control. They sit round him in a circle and try to stand up – but he has ordered them to stay seated. They find it impossible to go against his orders. **Right**: Glen Ford, a Hollywood actor hypnotized in 1978, who recounted several experiences of having lived in the past. The experiences upset him a great deal as the concept of reincarnation conflicted with his religious beliefs.

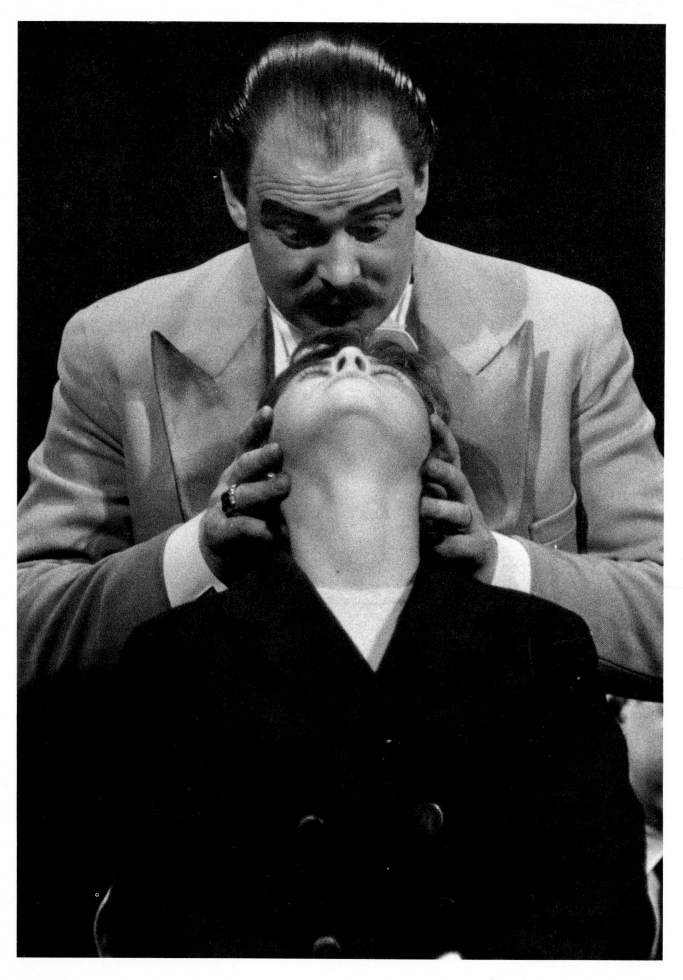

Proof of Reincarnation

Such cases have been widely accepted as proof of reincarnation. The terror shown by Jane Evans as she described the massacre and the screams of pain and fear that ended the Huxtable tape, as the soldier's leg was shot off in battle, were so convincing that even determined sceptics had to admit that it would have taken expert acting ability to fake such evidence. However, many psychologists prefer to believe that under hypnosis the subconscious mind may create a personality and background which the subject then plays out, as in a dream, drawing on subconscious memories to fill in the details.

The Finnish psychiatrist Dr Reima Kampman worked with a group of teenage school students who produced multiple personalities under hypnosis. One 13-year-old girl talked as Dorothy, the daughter of an English innkeeper who was born in 1139 near Norwich, giving a detailed account of life in England at the time, mentioning names and contemporary events and even singing a song in a language later recognized by experts as Middle English. The song was identified from records in the British Museum as the obscure 'Cuckoo Song'.

At the time, it seemed impossible to explain away such a feat on the part of a young teenager with very little knowledge of English history or language but seven years later, when she was re-hypnotized by Kampman, a different story emerged. Under hypnosis she recalled looking through a book called *The Story of Music* by Benjamin Britten and Imogen Holst in a library. One of the items in the book was the 'Cuckoo Song' and though she had only glanced at it briefly, her subconscious mind had filed away the entire song, in spite of the strange language.

Hypnosis and Mystery Solving

Police forces, particularly in the USA, have used hypnosis to unlock subconscious memories as an aid to solving crime. Witnesses able to give little useful information on a conscious level may yet sometimes produce a full description of a criminal or the numbers on a car licence plate under hypnosis.

Hypnosis shed new light on the puzzle of Ansel Bourne's missing two months. Bourne, a carpenter and local preacher, left his home in Rhode Island, USA, on 17 January 1887 after drawing $551 from his bank. He went to visit his nephew in Providence to discuss buying some farm land but then disappeared.

Dual Personalities

On the morning of 14 March he woke with a jolt in a bed at the back of a small confectionery and stationery store in Norristown, Pennsylvania, with no idea how or why he came to be there. He discovered that he was known in the town as Albert John Brown, who had rented the store in early February and had then proceeded to run the business competently and attended the local Methodist church. Bourne remembered nothing from the moment he had left his nephew's home 370 km (230 miles) away and could never explain why he had set up as a storekeeper, a business in which he had no experience or interest.

Three years later Bourne was hypnotized by Professor William James of Harvard and immediately became Albert John Brown, describing his journey from Pennsylvania on 17 January and the setting up of his shop. He was confused about his life before that date and could remember little after 13 March.

Professor James decided that Bourne and Brown were two distinct people, each with his own personality, mannerisms, gestures and handwriting. After more hypnotic treatment the personality of Bourne faded away, never to return. But how or why he had suddenly appeared to take over another man's life was never explained.

Hypnosis may help to solve mysteries but it has always remained something of a mystery itself. We do not fully understand how it works, so it has always been slightly suspect and much of its potential has been neglected.

Above: In the eighteenth and nineteenth centuries, street entertainers who hypnotized their subjects, were quite common. The hypnotist would gather an audience and provide them with 'amazing' spectacles involving the person hypnotized.
Left: Stage hypnotists have often obtained remarkable results in their performances. Here the hypnotist Tonelli works by suggestion on a young woman selected from a large group of people.

Glimpses of the Future

PROPHECIES FOR THEN AND NOW

NOSTRADAMUS

One of the most remarkable prophets of all time, Nostradamus, lived in southern France over 400 years ago. His predictions, couched in cryptic verses, brought him renown in his lifetime and have proved uncannily accurate.

He was born Michel de Nostradame in St Remy de Provence on 14 December 1503 and from boyhood he was fascinated by astrology. His family thought medicine was a more respectable career and he became a skilled physician, far ahead of his time with his concern for sanitation. Despite his skills, he was unable to save his own wife and children when they were stricken with bubonic plague and, disillusioned, he took to wandering through Europe, exercising his gift for prophecy.

Visions of the Future

His predictions were received sometimes with wonder, sometimes with scepticism. On a road near Ancona, in Italy, he was passing a group of Franciscan monks when he suddenly knelt in the mud in front of one of them, Brother Peretti, until recently a swine-herd. When questioned, Nostradamus explained: 'I must yield myself and bend a knee before his Holiness.' It was 40 years later, 19 years after Nostradamus himself was dead, that Brother Peretti became Pope Sixtus V.

Nostradamus longed to share his visions of the future but feared persecution as a sorcerer. As a precaution, when he published the first volume of his almanac in 1550, he veiled his prophecies in four-line poems called quatrains. This was an instant success and over the next few years he produced a total of 10 volumes containing 1,000 predictions, called *The Centuries*.

His accurate prophecy of the death of Henri II of France made him famous throughout the courts of Europe. His quatrain spoke of a 'young lion' overcoming an older one in single combat: 'In a golden cage, he will pierce the eye; two

wounds in one, then he dies a cruel death.' In 1559 Henri was taking part in a joust with a young soldier when his opponent's lance penetrated his gilt visor, blinding him and penetrating his brain. He died after several days of terrible pain.

Since then, every century has produced more evidence of Nostradamus's prophetic skills. Several of his verses describe the French Revolution, when 'Princes and lords are held captive in prisons' and he gives a vivid picture of the attempted flight of Louis XVI and his wife Marie Antoinette, taking a devious route 'by the forest of Reines', describing 'the queen white stone' and the 'monk-king in grey in Varennes'.

He forecast the plague that ravaged London in 1665 and the Great Fire of London in 1666, the rise of Napoleon and man's landing on the moon, walking on 'the corner of Luna'. Even more impressive are verses where he names people. Medical scientist Louis Pasteur is there, 'Pasteur will be renowned as a godlike man' as well as General de Gaulle, 'three times one surnamed de Gaulle will lead France.' The names of the leaders of the Second World War are mentioned: Duce, Franco and Hitler (though he calls him Hister):

In the mountains of Austria near the Rhine
There will be born of simple parents
A man who will claim to defend Poland and Hungary
And whose fate will never be certain.

The End of the World?

His most sombre prediction is a war to end all wars when he uses the latitude of New York City to predict: 'the sky will burn at 45 degrees, fire approaches the New City.' The end of the civilized world will come in: '1999 and seven months, when from the sky will come the great king of terror.'

MICHEL NOSTRADAMUS.
Médecin,
Né à S.ᵗ Remy, en Provence, le 14 Décemb 1503
Mort le 2 juillet 1566.

Michel Nostradamus, considered by many to be the foremost prophet of all time, made predictions which have proved to be astonishingly accurate.

MOTHER SHIPTON

Visitors to Knaresborough in Yorkshire still visit the small cave in the hillside where England's most famous prophetess, Mother Shipton, was born as Ursula Southeil in 1488.

Most of what is known about her comes from local tradition and 17th century pamphlets but it seems that her mother, Agatha, who had been hounded out of her home by local people because they suspected her of witchcraft, took refuge in the cave and died giving birth.

From the beginning Ursula was amazingly ugly and, possibly because of her terrible appearance, strange tales were told about her from babyhood. It was said that she could levitate herself and her cradle, that furniture moved around the cottage of its own accord and that

unfriendly neighbours were made to dance in circles, jabbed by invisible pins, until they dropped from exhaustion. Her nurse needed no light but the baby's nose, which was: 'of unproportionate length with many crooks and turnings, adorned with great pimples and which, like vapours of brimstone, gave strong lustre in the night.'

An Understanding Hag

By the time she reached her teens, Ursula looked like the caricature of a witch: abnormally tall, in spite of her hunched back, with an enormous hooked nose and great hairy warts on her chin. In spite of the persecution she suffered from local people who kept demanding that she should be burnt as a witch she had, according to a local priest, an 'extraordinary understanding' of others.

Perhaps that was how she managed to find a husband, in spite of her appearance. There is no record of who Toby Shipton was or where he came from but he married Ursula in 1512 and they had nine children, none of whom inherited Ursula's unfortunate looks.

By the time of her marriage she was

firmly established as a fortune-teller and as soon as a local girl was in her teens she would secretly visit Mother Shipton's home to find out the name of her future husband. Her predictions of the future were so accurate that her fame soon spread and many well-known people of the day consulted her.

Visions of the Future

Her prophecies of events, sometimes centuries in the future, became legend. First published in 1641, many have been added over the years, often with hindsight. Whenever there was a local disaster, someone who was sure to claim that Mother Shipton had foreseen it, and a brand new prophecy would be invented on the spot.

Tradition has established her as a seer who foretold Henry VIII's defeat of the French, the Caesarian birth of Edward VI, the reign of a maiden Queen (Elizabeth I) and the English Civil War.

She foresaw the execution of the unfortunate Lady Jane Grey after her nine days on the throne: 'A vertuous Lady then shall die, for being raised up too high'; and the beheading of Mary Queen of Scots: 'A widowed Queen in England shall be headless seen.'

Her fame was at its height in 1666 when one of her well-known prophecies had been fulfilled: the Great Fire of London. Samuel Pepys, in his diary, talks about the great excitement generated because 'Shipton's prophecy was out'.

In later centuries, some of her verses seem to foretell the Crimean War and the Klondike gold rush:

A house of glass shall come to pass
in England but, alas!
War will follow with the work
In the land of the Pagan and Turk
Gold shall be found, and found
In a land that's not now known.

Her glimpses into the 20th century seem uncanny, with their visions of cars and iron ships, but a man called Charles Hindley claimed that he had embroidered on the original prophecies to sell the edition published in 1862:

Carriages without horse shall go
And accidents fill the world with woe.
Iron in the water shall float
As easily as does a wooden boat.

Mother Shipton, born Ursula Southeil, although deemed very ugly (as the picture on the left portrays her) was nevertheless thought to be very kind and understanding of other people. She became established as a fortune-teller and her predictions of the future have proved extremely accurate.

JEANE DIXON

Even at the age of nine Jeane Dixon, from Washington in the United States, was seeing into the future. Later, as an ordinary housewife married to a real estate agent, she became renowned for her startling accuracy.

Predicting the Deaths of the Kennedys

In 1952 she predicted the assassination of John F. Kennedy 11 years ahead, at a time when Kennedy was still a senator for Massachusetts. She was in St Matthew's Cathedral in Washington one morning when she had a vision of the White House and a young, blue-eyed man standing at the door and, at the same time, heard a warning that a Democrat who would be inaugurated as President in 1960 would be assassinated while in office. Her prediction was reported but later forgotten.

In 1960 John F. Kennedy became the youngest man ever elected President, on the smallest majority of the popular vote. Early in 1963 Jeane Dixon began to have new, disturbing premonitions about the President's safety and she made several attempts to warn him of the danger she saw ahead. On the morning of Friday, 22 November, she told friends: 'This is the day it will happen.' That afternoon, Kennedy was riding in an open car through Dallas, Texas, when he was gunned down.

Five years later Jeane Dixon was addressing a meeting in the Ambassador Hotel in Los Angeles when a questioner asked if Robert Kennedy would ever become President. 'No,' she answered. 'He will never become President of the United States because of a tragedy right here in this hotel.'

A week later Robert Kennedy won the California primary and he had just finished addressing a victory rally from the stage of the Ambassador Hotel's ballroom when he was shot by a 24-year-old Jordanian born immigrant. He died the following day.

Clairvoyant Powers

Mrs Dixon has impressed many celebrities and statesmen with her clairvoyant powers. Comedian Bob Hope once tried to test her skills by asking how many strokes he had made during a game of golf earlier in the day. He made no mention of his partner in the game, as this was meant to be a closely guarded secret, but she answered without hesitation: 'You took 92 strokes and President Eisenhower took 96.'

Sadly, her warnings of tragedy ahead are not always heeded. In January 1942 she told the film actress Carole Lombard that it would be dangerous for her to travel by plane within the next six weeks. Carole, who was intensely patriotic, was going on a government-sponsored tour to sell war bonds at a victory rally in Indianapolis in three days' time and was not inclined to change her plans because of a clairvoyant's warning. The most she would agree to, when Jeane Dixon pressed, was to flip a coin: if it was heads she would cancel the trip, if it was tails, she would go ahead. The coin came down tails.

Carole reached Indianapolis safely and, as she was due to return by train, it looked as though the warnings were meaningless. Then at the last minute she took an overnight plane. At a stopover in Albuquerque Carole and her companion were asked if they would give up their seats to army officers who needed to join their unit but Carole, who had left after a blazing row with her husband Clark Gable, was anxious to get home to make up with him. She never reached him; near Las Vegas the plane ran into a violent storm and crashed in the mountains. The 90 m (300 ft) sheet of flame from the crashed aircraft was visible for miles.

We must hope that all Mrs Dixon's prophecies are not as accurate as the one she gave Carole Lombard. She has forecast a Third World War beginning in the late 1980s and culminating in 1999 – the same year given by Nostradamus for the end of the world.

Jeane Dixon, a modern-day prophet, proved uncannily accurate in her predictions. Long before John Kennedy became President of the USA she foretold his death: he was shot several times as he was riding in an open car in Dallas, Texas, on 22 November, 1963. Jeane Dixon is seen here with her famous crystal ball about which she says: 'I like to dream into it with lighted candles casting shadows behind me. When I sit here I can read people's minds.'

Prophetic Dreams

WARNINGS FOR THE FUTURE

The American writer Mark Twain dreamed that he saw the dead body of his brother, Henry, laid out on a burial casket with a bunch of white flowers on his breast, with a single red rose at its centre. It was so vivid that he woke still convinced that his brother was dead; the realization that he had been dreaming came as a great relief.

His relief was short-lived. The message came that Henry, who has been working in the boiler-room of a steamboat near Memphis, had been killed in an explosion. Twain journeyed to Memphis to find his brother laid out exactly as he had pictured him in the dream, except that there were no white flowers. As he stood there, a woman brought a large white bouquet with one red rose at the centre and laid it on Henry's breast.

In May 1812 John Williams, a Cornish tin mine manager, dreamed that he was standing in the lobby of the House of Commons when he saw a small man in a blue coat and white waistcoat shot by another man, dressed in a brown coat with decorative yellow buttons. When he asked who was shot, he was told that it was the Prime Minister, Spencer Perceval.

After dreaming the same dream three times he was so worried that he wanted to warn the Prime Minister but his friends dissuaded him, certain that he would be thought mad. Eight days later Perceval was assassinated in the lobby of the House of Commons.

Prophecies as Coincidences?

One of the favourite explanations for prophetic dreams is that they are merely coincidences – after all, the possibility of assassination might well figure in dreams about any President at any time. The same explanation is put forward for predictions of airline crashes, the argument being that many of us have dreamed of an airline crash, but that the dreams that fail to coincide with an actual event are forgotten.

Such an easy explanation would not satisfy David Booth, an American office manager who had the same dream night after night in May, 1979: he saw an American Airlines plane, on the point of take-off, roll over and crash to the

ground in flames. The dream was so real that he even felt the heat of the fire. After seven nights with the same dream re-occurring, he rang the airline officials and described it to them.

The day after an American Airlines DC10 crashed on take-off at Chicago airport on 25 May, killing 273 people, David Booth's nightmares stopped. The crash had happened exactly as he had pictured it in his dream.

When the great coal waste tip of Aberfan slid down the mountainside on to the south Wales village in 1966, killing nearly 150 people, most of them school-children, many people claimed that they had had premonitions of the disaster. One of the children who died, Eryl Mai Jones, had told her mother that she

AD IN HORROR

● More pictures on Pages 10, 13 and Back Page

LATE NEWS

● Rescuers pause as a casualty is brought out of the wreckage.

dreamed of walking to school only to find that it was no longer there: 'something black had come down all over it.' A London psychiatrist, Dr John Barker, investigated more than 60 claims and found that over 20 had been reported to other people before the fateful day and, though none of them corresponded exactly with the event itself, they were genuine enough to add up to evidence for some form of precognition.

This type of prophetic dream has led some researchers to think that a central clearing house should collect reports of premonitions and issue warnings where necessary. Bureaux have been set up at various times in several countries but so far there is no evidence that they have been able to prevent tragedies.

Above: Mark Twain, the American humorist and writer, was also a prophetic dreamer who dreamed of the death of his brother, Henry, shortly before the death actually occured. Details of his dream, which depicted the dead body of his brother laid out on a burial casket, bore an uncanny resemblance to the actual scene.

Faith Healing

MIRACLE CURES

Every year, as many as three million people flock to Lourdes, the great pilgrimage centre in France, in the hope of a cure for every ailment in the medical textbook. Thousands return home claiming that they are restored to health.

Ever since a poor peasant girl, Bernadette Soubirous, saw visions of the Virgin Mary in a grotto near the village of Lourdes in 1858, and at her command scrabbled in the mud to find a spring, cures have been reported by those who have bathed in the water. One of the first was the two-year-old son of Emperor Napoleon III, who was cured of severe sunstroke and threatened meningitis.

The Roman Catholic church takes a cautious line and only recognizes cures after the most rigorous investigation by its own Medical Bureau, when they are certain that the cure is permanent.

Since 1858, 65 cures have been officially recognized as 'miracles'. Among them was Evasio Ganora, suffering from Hodgkin's disease, so weak that he could do nothing but wait for death. When he was immersed in the cold water of the Lourdes baths he felt a powerful warmth running through him. He got up from his stretcher and walked back to the hospital, where he immediately started helping to carry other patients. When he got home to Italy, 37-year-old Ganora went back to work as a farm labourer.

Alice Couteault was dying slowly from disseminated sclerosis; at 35 she had wasted away to the point where she could no longer eat or dress herself. Her husband did not join the pilgrimage to Lourdes; he did not believe that anything could come of it until, waiting on the station for his wife to be carried from the train at the end of the trip, he saw her running down the platform towards him.

Healing was an integral part of the early Christian ministry, with Christ giving his disciples 'power and authority over all devils and to cure diseases'. Many saints, among them St Francis of Assisi, St Catherine of Siena and St Francis Xavier, are credited with miracle cures and relics of the saints were often prized for their healing properties.

But, though faith healing has always been closely associated with religious belief, faith is not a necessary element – except in so far as any treatment has a head start if the patient believes in it.

Above*: Crutches left at Lourdes by pilgrims who have been healed.*

Right*: Pilgrims in wheelchairs and on stretchers pray for miracles to happen.*

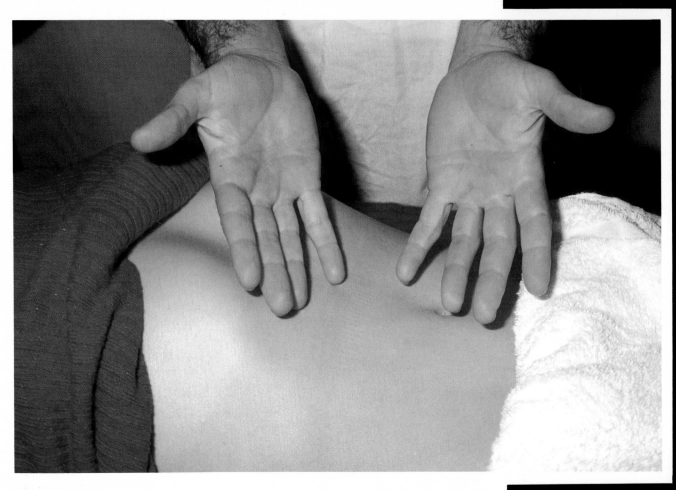

No Mental Barriers

Some of the pilgrims at Lourdes may be uplifted by religious fervour but the thousands of sick people who arrive at healing sessions every day, all over the world, are normally the medical rejects; they have exhausted all avenues of conventional medicine and this is a last resort. Healers often find they achieve the fastest results with small children or animals who put up no mental barriers and who have no psychological need to hang on to their illness.

Many healers are spiritualists, who believe that they act as a channel between this world and the spirit world and that the spirit of dead healers – whether a wise Indian medicine man or a great scientist like Louis Pasteur – direct or control them in their work.

The oldest and simplest method of healing is the laying on of hands, and many patients report a feeling of warmth or energy flooding through them at the moment of healing. However, contact between healer and patient is not essential and healers claim excellent results in helping people who may be hundreds, even thousands, of miles away.

Healers of the 20th century come in all guises. Some travel the world, their highly publicized rallies drawing people by the thousand, whipping up a frenzy of excitement that is often cited as producing temporary 'cures', with symptoms apparently disappearing only to return within days or even hours. Far more work quietly in their own communities, making no dramatic claims.

Children as Healers

Occasionally a child, too young to understand fully what is happening, appears to have genuine healing powers. When Linda Martel was only a toddler she could cure her father's headache and her brother recovered from gastric flu when she laid her hands on him. Linda was handicapped with spina bifida and died at the age of five, in 1961, and by then she was internationally famous. Cures were reported long after her death, from people who asked her family for a scrap of her dress or soil from her grave.

Psychic Surgery

One of the strangest and most hotly disputed forms of healing is psychic surgery, where the healer apparently performs operations with his bare hands, or perhaps with an ordinary knife, removing tumours from the body, then closing up the wound instantly. Though there is plenty of blood, the patient feels no pain

and the wound leaves no scar.

The best known psychic surgeon was the Brazilian José Arigo, who worked under a spirit control, Dr Fritz, a German doctor who had died in 1918. His first operation was in 1956, when a Brazilian senator claimed that he was cured after Arigo removed a tumour from his colon. Arigo's fame spread so that thousands of people flocked to his small town and he performed dozens of operations a day, often under the watchful eye of sceptical doctors and surgeons. Many were impressed, though mystified.

Since then psychic surgery has fallen into disrepute. In 1979 a BBC Nationwide programme showed a film of two psychic surgeons at work, with a commentary from a professional magician who demonstrated how the 'operations' could have been faked. It also produced the analysis of blood from towels used at the operation and from the patients' clothing, showing that it was pig's blood. However scathing the criticism, there are still plenty of people who claim that psychic surgery has cured them of painful or life-threatening complaints.

Proof for the Healing

Obtaining any scientific proof of the process of healing, under laboratory conditions, is very difficult but a few attempts have been made. A Canadian research biologist, Dr Bernard Grad, experimented with two groups of mice, all with small nicks in their skin. He found that the rate of healing in the group treated by a healer was significantly faster than that of the control group.

The medical profession as a whole has remained resistant to the idea that any form of faith or spirit healing can effect a cure but more and more doctors are recognizing that our emotional and mental state plays a significant role in our susceptibility to disease and in the likelihood of recovery. They are well aware of the 'placebo' effect, whereby patients can get better on a course of pills that contain nothing more potent than sugar, simply because they believe the doctor will make them well.

Far left: Psychic surgery is regarded as one of the strangest forms of faith healing. It is hotly disputed by many medical experts who claim the 'operations' performed are fakes.
Left: A faith healer at work.

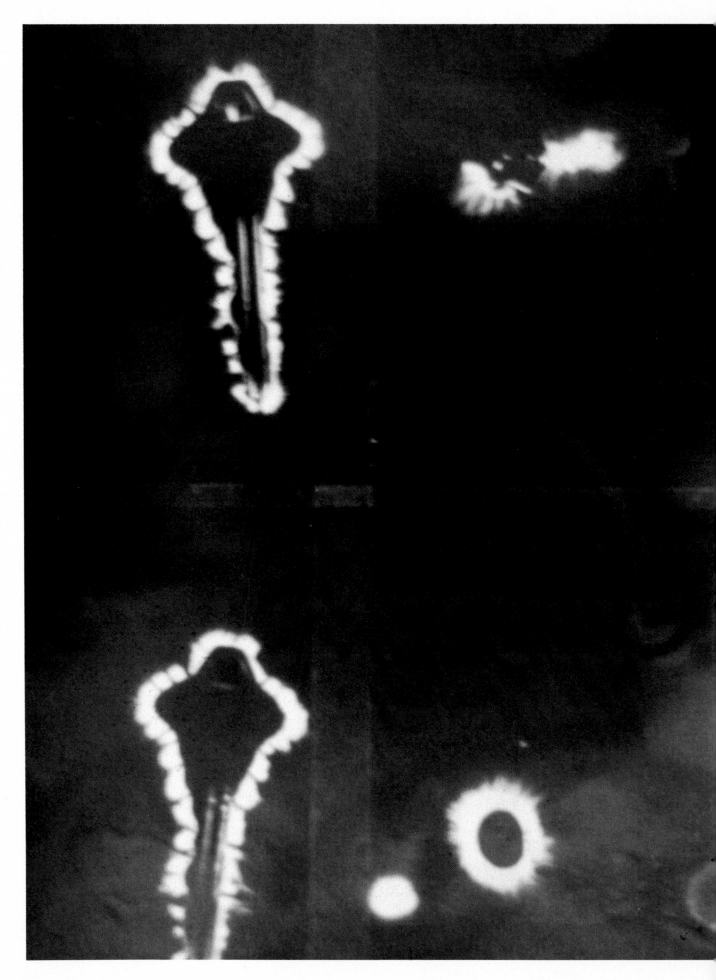

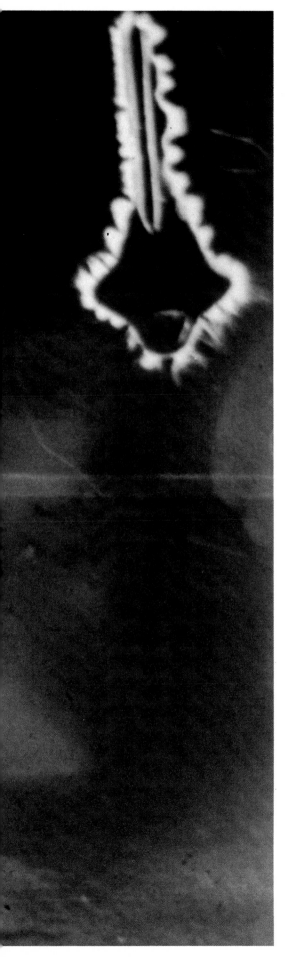

Mind Over Matter

BENDING METAL OBJECTS

On 23 November 1973, Uri Geller appeared for the first time on British television. He held a fork to his hand, stroking it gently until it bent and then broke. He rubbed his fingers across the glass of broken watches and they began ticking. After the broadcast the BBC switchboard was jammed with calls reporting bent cutlery or re-started watches and clocks from all over the country.

A Sunday newspaper followed this up by announcing a set time when Geller would be concentrating his powers and asked readers to report anything that happened. They recorded 300 bent spoons and forks, 1,000 broken clocks and watches starting up again.

Opinion regarding the phenomena was sharply divided: Was Geller a conjurer or a genuine psychic? Was his performance just a trick played on a gullible public or a genuine demonstration of psychokinesis, moving objects by the power of mind? Some sceptics dismissed the whole thing as mass hallucination, though that made it hard to explain away the permanent bends in metal implements.

Tests for Uri Geller

Geller had already undergone tests at Stanford Research Institute in California, supervised by two physicists. They had made a filmed record of Geller's effect on a Bell gaussmeter, an instrument measuring magnetic fields. By passing his hands near the gaussmeter he was able to achieve a full scale deflection of the instrument several times, indicating that his magnetic field was at least half as strong as that of the earth.

In the next few years he underwent tests at 17 different laboratories. Some of the most thorough testing was carried out in Britain by two academics from London University, Professor John Taylor of King's College and Professor John Hasted of Birkbeck College.

Above: Uri Geller is seen (left) with Jimmy Young inspecting the Automobile Association's telephone box key which bent during Geller's appearance on Young's BBC Radio 2 programme in October 1974.
Left: A Kirlian photograph, showing Uri Geller's ability to bend keys with psychic energy.

British Tests

Geller was often accused of bending metal by sheer pressure, so he was asked to bend a brass strip attached to a letter balance which would register the exact amount of pressure he exerted. As he stroked the strip the scale read only 15 grams (½ oz), but the strip bent upwards, against the pressure of his fingers.

Another experiment involved influencing a Geiger counter. When the instrument was held near him, the count was zero. When Geller held it in his hands and concentrated hard, the needle deflected to 50 counts per second and its gentle bleeping sound rose to a wail, which would normally indicate dangerously radioactive material. When he stopped concentrating, the wailing stopped. After several attempts, Geller was able to deflect the needle to 1,000 counts per second, with the machine screaming.

James Randi

In spite of some impressive results, many people remained convinced that 'the Geller effect' was achieved by simple conjuring tricks. Chief among his detractors was the American magician James Randi, who maintained that scientists were easily fooled by a clever performer.

When a parapsychology laboratory was set up at Washington University in Missouri, Randi sent along two young helpers who pretended that they had discovered psychic powers. The investigators were amazed by their abilities as they bent objects in sealed containers and twisted keys, until they revealed that they achieved all their results by trickery, undermining what seemed like careful monitoring by distracting their observers and claiming that film cameras sapped their powers.

Scientific Testing

Two researchers from the University of Bath, Dr Brian Pamplin and Dr Harry Collins, tested a group of children who had bent metal at home, following Geller's broadcast. The children were in a room with an observer, who was told to glance away at certain times, while scientists watched with keen attention through one-way mirrors. Once the children thought no one was looking, they cheated: one put a rod under his foot, others used two hands and as much strength as they could muster. After-

wards the researchers stated: 'We can assert that in no case did we observe a rod or spoon bent other than by palpably normal means.'

These exposures undermined confidence in scientific testing. However, among the rash of twisted forks and headless spoons appearing when Geller fever was at its height, there were some feats that seemed inexplicable. For instance, a 12-year-old girl managed to bend a metal towel rail 5 mm (¼ inch) in diameter at an angle of 40 degrees as her parents watched. The rail was made of mild steel with a chromium plate finish and later tests showed that bending it would have taken the force of at least a quarter of a ton.

Serious attempts at investigating the field of psychokinesis began in the 1930s when Joseph Banks Rhine set up the world's first laboratory for the study of parapsychology in North Carolina. He attempted to investigate claims from a professional gambler that it was possible to influence the fall of dice by willpower but, though the results attracted a lot of attention, he was criticized for his lack of scientific safeguards.

In a long-running American project, the Society for Research into Rapport and Telekinesis devised a system of minilabs. At first, these consisted of wooden boxes with glass lids. Various objects would be placed inside the box, and a layer of coffee grounds spread across the floor before it was locked and sealed in the presence of witnesses. Members of the group would then concentrate on the objects, trying to move one across the floor of the box. The coffee grounds made sure that no one could shake or tilt it; after a successful experiment there would be a single trail across the box to mark the path of the chosen object.

Later a perspex minilab was developed, so that what happened inside could be recorded by cine camera. However, the resulting film of levitating pens and objects moving across the floor of the box have been disputed by psychic researchers who have produced films of their own to show how the evidence could have been faked.

Solid proof is hard to find but many sincere researchers are convinced that the power of mind over matter does exist, perhaps as a result of tapping a reservoir of energy that is all around us.

Right: A spoon bent by Uri Geller. The energy required to produce such an unnatural bend must have been considerable.
Below: A Kirlian photograph of Uri Geller's index finger during a burst of energy which shows the considerable force generated.

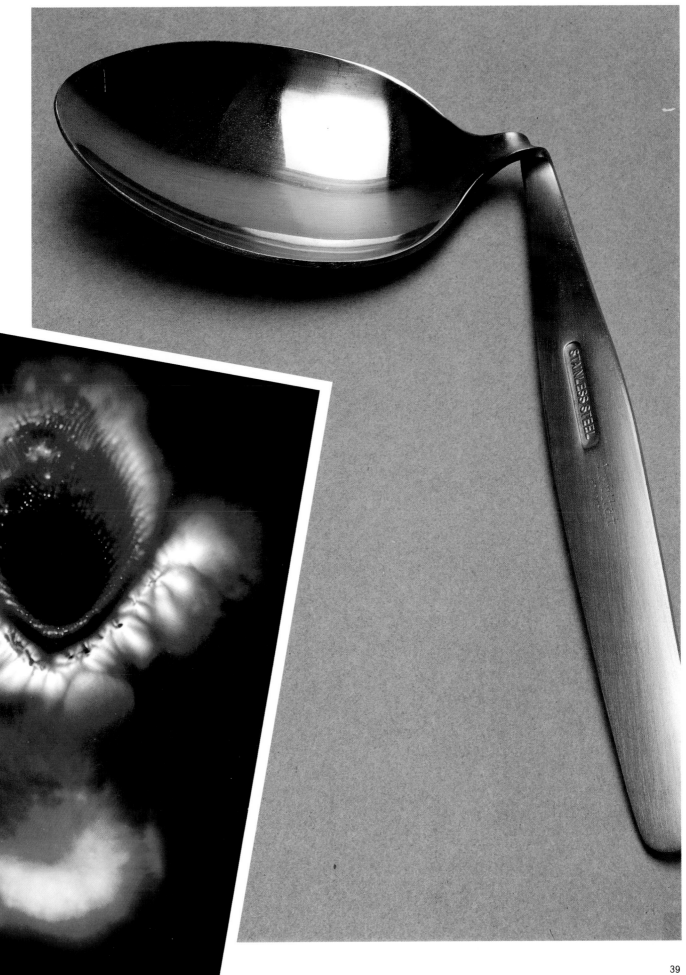

CHAPTER TWO

HUMAN MYSTERIES

◆

Human mysteries defy all reason and make us doubt the evidence of our own senses. Can we believe our eyes when we see bodies rise into the air unaided or non-existent wounds begin to bleed? Men walk across pits of fire with unburned feet, yet bodies burst into flames of their own accord and are incinerated within minutes, while the room around them remains untouched.

We can speculate and argue over the disappearance of an entire ship's crew or an incredible chain of coincidences but there are some happenings that refuse to conform to the normal laws of nature.

Left: *'Silent Pool' at Newlands Corner being dragged by the police in the vain search for the body of Agatha Christie who had disappeared days before.*

Spontaneous Human Combustion

BURSTING INTO FLAMES

Left: All that remained of Dr. John Irving Bentley: the lower half of his right leg with the slipper still on it. Below: Spontaneous human combustion of Mrs Mary Reeser of St Petersburg, Florida, in 1951.

Spontaneous human combustion, when a person's body bursts into flames for no apparent reason and burns at such a high temperature that it is reduced to ashes within a few minutes, is one of the most baffling phenomena ever to face forensic scientists.

The Burning of Bodies

On a cold December morning in 1966 a meter reader, Mr Gosnell, arrived at the home of a retired doctor, John Irving Bentley, in Coudersport, Pennsylvania. He knew that 92-year-old Bentley could only get about with the aid of a walking frame so he let himself in and went straight down to the meters in the basement. There he noticed a strange smell and a light blue smoke so he went upstairs to investigate. He found the bedroom smoky but empty so he peeped into the bathroom – and received the shock of his life. Beside a blackened hole in the floor lay Dr Bentley's steel walking frame and the lower half of his right leg with the slipper still on it. Apart from that, all that was left of the doctor was a pile of ashes on the basement floor below. Gosnell ran from the building yelling: 'Dr Bentley is burned up!'

The coroner recorded a verdict of 'death by asphyxiation and 90 per cent burning of the body'. The first obvious explanation was that Dr Bentley had set himself on fire while lighting his pipe but this hardly explained why his pipe was carefully placed on its stand by the bed or why a fire of such ferocity had done so little damage to the surrounding area; the rubber tips of the walking frame, as they lay across the hole in the floor, were still intact and the nearby bathtub was hardly scorched.

Another victim was Mary Reeser, a plump 67-year-old widow who lived alone in St Petersburg, Florida. A telegram arrived for her on 2 July 1951, but when her landlady tried to deliver it she found the handle of the apartment door too hot to touch. She summoned help from workmen who broke down the door but inside, in spite of intense heat, there was no fire. They found Mrs Reeser's armchair burned down to the springs but all that remained of the widow was a few charred bones, a skull shrunk the size of a baseball and an untouched left foot, burned off at the ankle.

Dr Wilton Krogman, a forensic specialist who investigated the Reeser case, said that it would have taken a heat of about 1,650°C (3,000°F) to melt bone in this way and such a fire should have burned the whole apartment. He also pointed out that the smell of such a cremation would normally have spread through the entire building.

A small area of carpet around the chair was charred, there was soot on the walls and ceiling above and two candles about 3.6 m (12 ft) from the body had melted. A newspaper near the chair and the linen on the bed were both unscorched.

All sorts of theories were put forward: a flame-thrower had been used to murder her; she had poured petrol over herself and set light to it; the body had been burned elsewhere then taken back to the apartment where someone had arranged the room to look as though an accident had taken place. None of these theories, however, seemed to fit all the facts.

Questioning Spontaneous Combustion

Though many doctors still refuse to admit that spontaneous human combustion is possible, such extraordinary cases are nothing new. One of the first reported cases was in 1673, when a Parisian alcoholic was reduced to a pile of ash and a few finger bones, though the straw bed on which he was sleeping remained intact. In 1744, 60-year-old Grace Pett of Ipswich suddenly burst into flames in front of her horrified daughter who said that she burned 'like a log of wood consumed by fire'.

In such inexplicable cases, the fire is often confined to a very small area, with furnishings and even clothing left untouched. In 1841, the *British Medical Journal* reported a case described by Dr F. S. Reynolds. A 40-year-old woman, who seemed to have fallen near the hearth, was found while still burning. Incredibly, the bones of her leg were carbonized but her stockings remained undamaged.

Mrs Madge Knight of Aldingbourne, Sussex, woke in the early hours of one morning feeling as though she was burning. Her screams roused her husband and sister, who found that she had terrible burns on her back, though there was no smell of burning and no scorch marks on the bedclothes. Though some experts said that, because of the lack of any signs of fire, the burns must have been caused by some corrosive liquid, nothing was found in the house. Madge Knight was questioned many times before she died three weeks later from blood poisoning, but she was unable to shed any light on what had happened.

In the 19th century, doctors tended to believe that victims were heavy drinkers, so that the alcohol-soaked fat of their bodies made them easily combustible. Equally far-fetched was the notion of a curse, suggested in the case of Mr Temple Thurston, an English author who was found dead in his armchair, the lower half of his body badly burned though there was no sign of fire in the room. Supporters of the curse theory pointed out that the burns on his body looked as though he had been burned at the stake and that the flames had been put out before they reached the upper part of his body.

Incineration: the Facts?

A lecturer in forensic medicine at Leeds University, Dr D. J. Gee, investigated the case of an old lady found on the hearth in her living-room, her body completely burned except for the right foot. The furniture was black with soot and the paintwork blistered but there was very little other damage. A tea towel hanging over the oven door close to the body was hardly singed and dry firewood stacked inside the oven was untouched. Dr Gee put forward the idea that, when she fell on the hearth, cinders had set fire to her head and the body had gone on burning in its own fat like a candle, with the draught from the chimney drawing the flames up and preventing them from spreading to the rest of the room.

Some cases, where the victim has fallen on to a hearth below an open chimney, may conform to the human candle theory; many others do not. In 1904 Mrs Gladys Cochrane of Falkirk, Scotland, was found burned beyond recognition, still sitting in a chair surrounded by cushions and pillows. In 1957, Anna Martin was found completely incinerated in her home in West Philadelphia, yet the room was cold and there was no fire.

Above: An old soldier burnt in a hayloft in 1888 in Aberdeen; another example of spontaneous human combustion. **Right**: The spontaneous combustion of Krook in Dickens's Bleak House.

Fire-walking

WHEN MEN ARE NOT FOR BURNING

Fire-walking, when men walk over red-hot coals or lava without feeling pain or suffering burns, is one of the most dramatic and baffling of all human mysteries. It happens in India, Tibet, Japan, the Philippines and Malaysia and defies all attempts at rational explanation.

Fire-Walking Ceremonies

In Fiji, for instance, the fire-walk takes place across a pit 6 m (20 ft) wide, lined with burning logs and spread with stones so hot that they glow. Then a priest calmly leads a line of followers across, apparently conferring on each of them his own immunity to pain.

The same immunity is recorded in the bible story of Shadrach, Meshach and Abednego who were cast into the fiery furnace on the orders of King Nebuchadnezzar. The fire had no power to harm them: 'nor was a hair of their heads singed, neither were their coats damaged, nor had the smell of fire passed on them.'

Over the last 100 years many travellers have reported watching amazing firewalking ceremonies and some have found themselves joining in. A British professor, Edward Stephenson, was invited to join a fire-walk in Tokyo, when the participants strolled out on to the hot stones without any special preparation. The only injury Professor Stephenson sustained was a scratch from the sharp edge of one of the stones.

A New Zealand magistrate, Colonel Gudgeon, joined a Maori fire-walk in 1899 with great trepidation. He felt the tremendous heat, like walking across a hot oven, but the only effect on his feet was a gentle tingling feeling.

Even less willing was Dr W. T. Brigham of the British Museum, pressed by South Sea islanders to join them on a walk across the molten lava of a recently erupted volcano. Though they advised him to remove his boots he was too nervous and eventually they pulled him on to the lava, boots and all. As he walked across an area 46 m (50 yd) wide, his boots and socks were burned away but his feet remained unscathed.

All sorts of experiments have been tried by witnesses determined to solve this mystery. An American doctor, Harry

B. Wright, tested the feet of fire-walkers in Fiji immediately after the ceremony. When he pricked the soles of their feet with a pin, or touched them with a lighted cigarette, they flinched and yelped with pain, just like anyone else.

Dr T. Hocken proved to his complete satisfaction first that the fire was just as hot as it appeared, by suspending a thermometer over it, and that the feet of the walkers had not been specially toughened or treated in any way. He even licked them to make sure that no chemicals had been applied.

Harry Price's Experiment

In 1935 both *Nature* and *The Lancet* carried accounts of an experiment set up by Harry Price, one of Britain's best known psychical researchers, with a young Indian, Kuda Bux, in Carshalton, Surrey, with the help and supervision of physicists from the University of London. A 7 m (24 ft) fire pit was set up and its heat stoked up so that the surface temperature was 430°C (800°F).

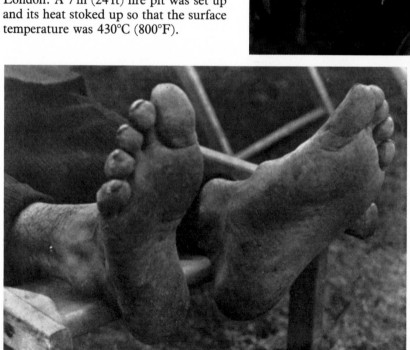

Above: The undamaged feet of a firewalker. **Right**: A dramatic photograph of a fire dance in Bali.

Kuda Bux

University experts examined the feet of Kuda Bux and a doctor washed and dried them, to eliminate any possibility of artificial aids; he also took their temperature and applied a small piece of sticking plaster to the sole of one foot.

Kuda Bux, who had made no special preparations, proceeded to walk the length of the trench four times. In between each walk all the ash was removed, in case it acted as insulation. Afterwards, when his feet were examined again, there was no sign of injury of blistering. The sticking plaster had not been burned and the temperature of Bux's feet had not risen.

Two spectators were brave enough to try to copy Bux. Both took a couple of steps at the very edge of the trench and both suffered badly blistered feet.

German scientists who ran tests during the famous fire-walk in Langadhas, in northern Greece, were just as perplexed at the end of their investigations. Each year, in May, the people of Langadhas commemorate the Emperor Constantine's miraculous feat in saving relics from a burning church without being touched by the flames. These fire-walkers prepare themselves by days of fasting and eventually emerge in what seems like a hypnotic trance, to walk on and off a fire with a surface temperature of 500°C (932°F) for as long as 20 minutes.

Scientists fastened thermocouples to the feet of several walkers to test the temperature and fastened electrodes to their heads, to monitor brain activity. They found that, in spite of the immense heat of the fire, the thermocouples measured a much lower temperature, 180°C (365°F). Though the brain scan for one of the walkers showed a high level of theta activity – the slow waves usually associated with deep sleep, which might be linked with the ability to ignore pain – the other walkers showed no change in their brain patterns.

Some scientists have put forward the theory that the ability to fire-walk is the result of long training, so that people who do this are able to walk so briskly that the soles of their feet are never in contact with the coals for longer than half a second and therefore have no time to burn. However, this does not explain how European visitors to fire-walking festivals have often been able to join the walk, so long as the leader invited them to do so, while those who have braved the coals on their own account usually find themselves badly burned.

Immunity from the effects of fire is not

confined to mystics or holy men. The Victorian medium Daniel Dunglas Home startled watchers at a seance by stirring the fire, then putting his face right into the hot coals, moving it from side to side as though it was in a basin of water. And he could share his immunity with others; when he handed round burning embers, no one was burned.

The writer Mrs Samuel Carter Hall had such faith in Home's abilities that she watched him place a lump of red-hot coal on her husband's head without the slightest fear. Her husband felt warmth but no heat while Home drew his white hair up over the coal, which could still be seen glowing through the strands.

Self Hypnosis?

One of the most popular explanations is some form of self-hypnosis, and a hypnotic suggestion passed on to followers. Hypnosis certainly allow doctors to perform painless surgery but the ability to stop such intense heat from having any physical effect is far more difficult to explain.

*Left: Walking through hot coals. Some form of self-hypnosis has been put forward to explain the lack of pain felt from the fire but this does not explain the ability to stop intense heat from having any physical effect. **Above**: A fire-walking ceremony in Greece. The women walk unhurriedly through the burning coals.*

The Turin Shroud
THE CLOTH THAT COVERED CHRIST

The Holy Shroud, housed in Turin Cathedral since the 16th century, was always said to be Christ's winding sheet as it bore the faint outlines of his body; however, the same claim has been made for other pieces of cloth in many other European churches.

It was only when the Turin Shroud was photographed for the first time in 1898 that, instead of faint outlines, the clear imprint of the face and body of a man emerged; the shroud itself seemed to be a kind of photographic negative.

The cloth itself is 434 cm (14 ft 2 in) long and 109 cm (3 ft 7 in) wide and shows the outline of a naked man 181 cm (6 ft) tall, with shoulder-length hair and a beard. He had been tortured and crucified: there are marks of a severe flogging and wounds where nails were driven through the wrists and where a single nail fastened both feet. There is also a wound on the right side, between the fifth and sixth ribs.

All the wounds are consistent with the description of Christ's crucifixion in the New Testament. There are even bruises on the shoulders which could have been made by carrying a heavy cross, lacerations on the knees from heavy falls and blood from scratches on the forehead which could have been caused by the crown of thorns thrust mockingly on to the head of the 'King of the Jews'. Medical evidence puts the age of the dead man between 30 and 45.

The early history of the shroud is uncertain. All that is known is that it arrived in France in the 14th century. It was owned by the Dukes of Savoy and kept in a special shrine, where it was damaged by fire in 1532. It was mended by nuns and eventually moved to Turin Cathedral in 1572.

No Scientific Proof

No scientific tests yet attempted have yielded conclusive proof that this is the shroud of the dead Christ but neither have they proved that it is any kind of fake.

No evidence of any type of pigment has showed up, so it seems impossible that the image could have been painted on the shroud. Analysis of the cloth has shown that it is of ancient Middle-Eastern origin and that some of the pollen it contained came from plants normally found around the Dead Sea in Palestine. The cloth shows the imprint of coins, placed on the eyes of the dead man, and in 1980 Professor Filas of Loyola University, Chicago, found that these had been made by Roman coins minted between AD 30 and AD 32, when Pontius Pilate governed Palestine.

The intriguing question of how the image came to be imprinted on the fabric so firmly that it has survived the centuries, has occupied many scientists. It may have been cause by gas, probably ammonia, from the skin mixing with the ritual burial spices but that would not explain why this particular shroud retains such unique clarity and detail.

Intense Radiation?

One scientist from the Santa Barbara Research Center described the process of forming the image as 'the boiling up of the surface material of the outer threads. Certain evidence indicates that this may have been caused by a violent burst of radiant heat.'

New Testament accounts say that when the disciples went to Christ's tomb they found the grave clothes but no body. It could be that a burst of intense radiation dissolved the body and left its imprint on the shroud.

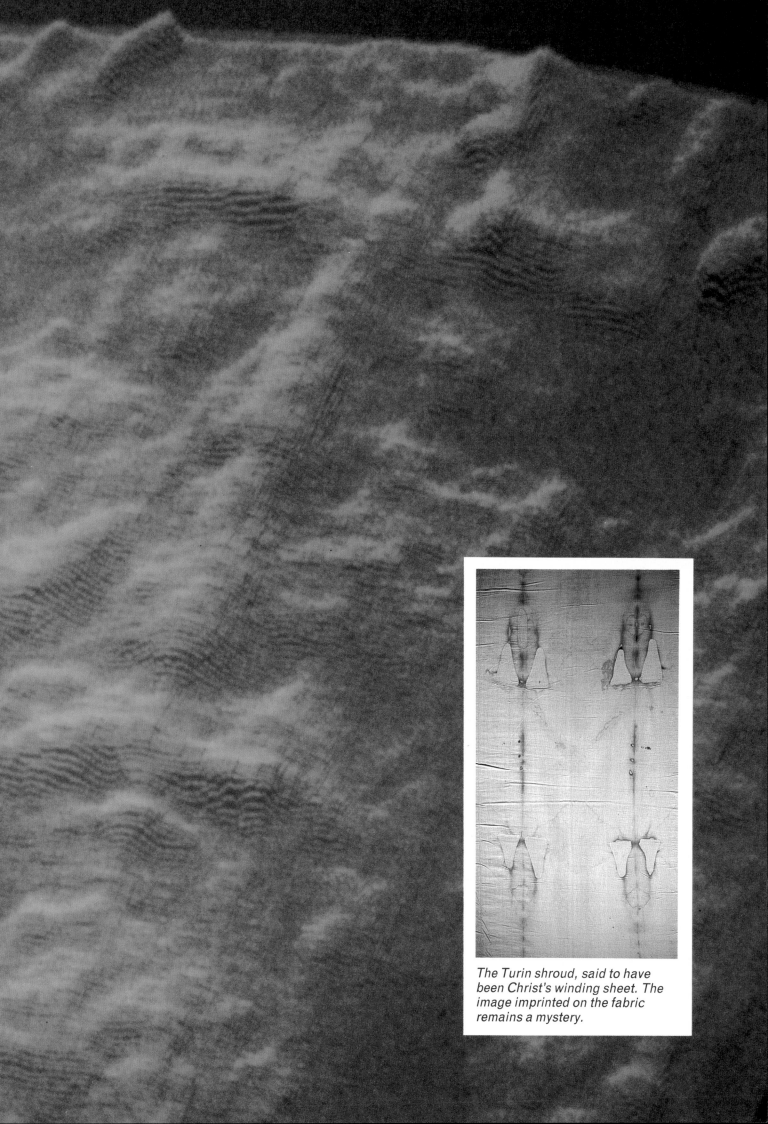

The Turin shroud, said to have been Christ's winding sheet. The image imprinted on the fabric remains a mystery.

Coincidences

FACT OR FICTION?

Coincidences are usually dismissed as events that seem to be connected but really happen by chance. Sometimes, however, a set of coincidences is so striking that chance seems too tame an explanation.

The Twenty-Year Cycle

American researchers instance the strange '20-year-cycle' of the elections and deaths of US presidents. Since 1840, every president elected at 20-year intervals has died in office:

William Henry Harrison, elected 1840, died 1841

Abraham Lincoln, elected 1860, assassinated 1861

James A. Garfield, elected 1880, assassinated 1881

William McKinley, elected 1900, assassinated 1901

Warren G. Harding, elected 1920, died 1923

Franklin D. Roosevelt, elected 1940, died 1945

John F. Kennedy, elected 1960, assassinated 1963

The next President in the cycle is Ronald Reagan, elected in 1980. Optimists hope that he will break the cycle because of his lucky escape from death when he was shot soon after his election.

Other Causes at Work

Normally we believe that the future is largely unpredictable because events depend on a subtle chain of cause and effect but astonishing coincidences like the '20-year-cycle' suggest that there might be some other, as yet unrecognized, principle at work. The Austrian biologist Paul Kammerer, who made the first systematic study of coincidence, thought that the coincidences we notice are only very few of those that do actually occur and that some cosmic force unconnected to cause and effect might be at work.

Since then Jung has formulated the principle of 'synchronicity' and has expounded complicated theories about its meaning for the human psyche – theories yet to be thoroughly investigated.

Meanwhile, coincidences fascinate re-searchers. John Littlewood, in his *Mathematician's Miscellany*, cites the instance of a girl trying to visit her sister, Florence Rose Dalton, a maid in a London house at 42 Walton Street. By mistake, the girl wandered into a neighbouring street and arrived at 42 Ovington Square instead. When she asked for Florence Rose Dalton she was told that though a maid of that name worked in the house she was on holiday at the moment and her sister was filling in until her return!

Coincidences as Prophecies

In the Second World War, when the Allies were planning the invasion of Normandy, the operation itself was known as Overlord and four other key code-words figured in the top-secret plans: Utah, Omaha, Mulberry and Neptune. Incredibly, all five words appeared in crossword clues in the *Daily Telegraph* in the four weeks before the invasion. British Intelligence officers descended on the newspaper, convinced that there was a spy at work, only to find that the compiler of the crosswords had chosen the words entirely by chance.

Some coincidences seem to border on precognition and the Jung theory indicates that premonitions might be part of the workings of the same unidentified natural force that governs coincidence. In 1898 Morgan Robertson published a novel about an 'unsinkable' luxury liner setting off from Southampton on its maiden voyage to New York but hitting an iceberg in the Atlantic and sinking with appalling loss of life because there were not enough life-boats. He called the ship the *Titan*. Fourteen years later, the 'unsinkable' *Titanic* sank in the same way in roughly the same place with the same tragic consequences.

Edgar Allen Poe, in 1837, wrote a story about four men adrift in an open boat after a shipwreck. They drew straws to decide who should be killed and eaten by the others and the cabin boy, Richard Parker, drew the short straw. Seven years later, after an actual shipwreck, four men faced with starvation as they drifted in an open boat also drew straws and the unlucky one was the cabin boy – whose name was Richard Parker!

Since 1840, every president of the United States elected at 20-year intervals has died in office, which would seem to be more than mere coincidence. **Above:** Benjamin Harrison, who was President for only one year (1840–1841) before his death. **Left:** President Lincoln's assassination by John Wilkes Booth in 1865.

The Bermuda Triangle
THE TRIANGLE OF DEATH

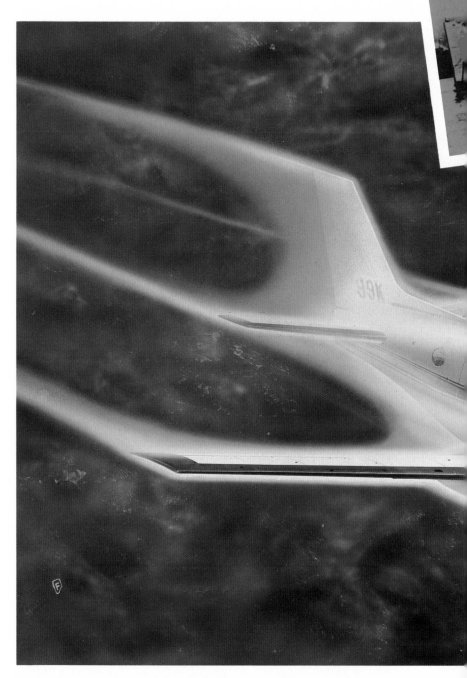

It has been called the Triangle of Death, the Devil's Triangle, the Graveyard of the Atlantic and the Hoodoo Sea. It is the notorious area of the Atlantic between the Florida coast of the United States, Bermuda and Puerto Rico: the Bermuda Triangle. Scores of ships and planes have vanished into thin air while travelling through it. They have disappeared without leaving wreckage or bodies, as if they had crossed over into a different dimension. The earliest recorded disappearance was the American Navy ship Cyclops, in 1918.

The Bermuda Triangle became part of legend in December 1945. Five Avenger torpedo-bombers set off on a routine training mission from their base in Fort Lauderdale, Florida. All the aircraft carried the latest navigation equipment, flying conditions were ideal and Flight 19 began smoothly but after an hour and a half the control tower heard Flight Instructor Lieutenant Charles G. Taylor saying anxiously: 'This is an emergency. We seem to be off course. We cannot see land – repeat – we cannot see land.'

'Which Way is West?'

The control tower instructed him to head due west but the reply came: 'We don't know which way is west. Everything is wrong, strange. We aren't sure of any direction. Even the ocean doesn't look as it should.'

The last words heard from any of the aircraft was when one of the pilots was trying to contact the flight instructor, five hours after their departure on a mission scheduled to take two hours. By then the weather had deteriorated and heavy seas were reported. The giant Martin Mariner sea plane, with a crew of 13, was sent on a rescue mission but after 20 minutes radio contact was lost. In all, 6 planes and 27 men disappeared.

The Limbo of the Lost

A journalist, Vincent Gaddis, first gave the area its name, calling it 'The Deadly Bermuda Triangle' in an article for an American adventure magazine. Later he collated the strange disappearances in the area for a book, *Invisible Horizons*. They added up, he said, to a 'total far beyond the laws of chance' and he went on to speculate on a 'vast unknown – the same misty limbo of the lost feared by our forefathers' and even that a 'spacetime continua may exist around us on the earth, interpenetrating our known world'.

Above: *Many strange effects have been noticed by pilots flying over the Bermuda Triangle: this plane developed a strange glow.*

from radar screens in the Miami control tower for 10 minutes, then reappear and land safely – with every clock and watch on board 10 minutes slow. Unfortunately, the story is short on facts and there is no convincing evidence that this ever happened.

Pilots have recorded being shaken, as though a giant hand had grabbed hold of them, and the crew of one ship said that the boilers went wild as the ship tossed on non-existent waves, as if an invisible force was trying to rip the vessel apart.

Magnetic Disturbances

Though the US Coast Guard has always opposed the whole idea of the 'deadly Bermuda Triangle', their records show inexplicable happenings, in this heavily travelled area. In December 1975 the Coast Guard cutter *Diligence* was on the way to assist a burning freighter when the radio and navigation equipment broke down completely. At the same time the crew saw mysterious green lights falling from the sky. Later investigations found that these lights could not have been flares and revealed no reason for the equipment failure. In the previous year, the crew of the Coast Guard cutter *Hollyhock* saw a huge land mass on their radar, where no real land existed. Once again, no fault could be found on the radar equipment.

Don Henry, the captain of the salvage tug *Good News*, sailing from Puerto Rico to Fort Lauderdale in 1966, was called to the bridge to investigate when the compass started spinning. All the boat's electrical equipment suddenly failed and it seemed to be swallowed up in a thick bank of fog, rolling in rough water. Then, just as suddenly, the boat came out of the fog into a clear day and calm sea, its compass behaving normally.

Aircraft pilots have encountered similar problems. Chuck Wakely, was flying from Nassau to Miami in 1964 when he saw a faint glow a 'localized fuzzy light' around the wings of his plane. As the intensity of the light increased, his instruments began to malfunction. It was only when the glow faded again that they worked normally once more.

Scientists still do not understand fully the workings of the earth's magnetic field and a number of similar reports of magnetic disturbances affecting the behaviour of instruments have come from other areas. It seems highly likely that some pocket of energy exists within the Triangle, affecting the performance of instruments and contributing to the loss of shipping and aircraft.

Top: The United States Navy cargo ship Cyclops, which disappeared on her way to Baltimore in March 1918, with more than three hundred people on board.

Since then there have been many theories: subterranean volcanoes, space-time warps, black holes, even aliens descending in flying saucers to gather up human specimens caught in 'vortices' where normal gravity does not apply.

The legend has undoubtedly grown with the publicity. An Eastern Airlines plane was supposed to have vanished

Levitation
DEFYING THE PULL OF GRAVITY

Reports of levitation, when a human being rises into the air for several minutes at a time without any physical means being employed, come from all over the world, from time immemorial – far too many instances for them all to be dismissed as fakes or hallucinations.

Mystical Levitation

Religious ecstasy has been the cause in some cases, like St Teresa of Avila who often floated for several minutes while she was praying, in full view of the other nuns. During communion, she had to cling on to the grille in front of her to keep herself on the ground. At first, this frightened her so much that she asked the nuns to hold her down and forbade witnesses to talk about it. When she described the experience later she admitted that it gave her a feeling of great sweetness if she did not resist but: 'It seemed to me, when I tried to make some resistance, as if a great force beneath my feet lifted me up ... After the rapture was over, I have to say my body seemed frequently to be buoyant, as if all weight had departed from it, so much that now and then I scarcely knew that my feet touched the ground.'

In the 17th century, the church did its best to suppress reports of the flights of Joseph of Copertino but scores of people, including Pope Urban VIII, saw him float into the air. Joseph was a feeble-minded peasant boy accepted as a lay brother by a Franciscan order who scourged and starved himself in the hope of achieving a state of ecstasy. He was so successful that he frequently rose into the air above the heads of his fellow monks at mass. Once he floated to the high altar, where he remained among the lighted candles for 15 minutes, oblivious to the pain of the burns.

For most of his monastic life Joseph was banned from attending mass because of the disruption he caused but this did not stop his levitations. The other monks had to bring a ladder to fetch him down from an olive tree in the garden, where he was stranded after one period of ecstasy was over. Even the doctor who attended his deathbed found him hovering a few inches above it.

Levitation and Transcendental Meditation

Students of transcendental meditation claim that they can learn to cancel the effects of gravity through meditation and mental discipline. One student described the technique: 'People would rock gently, then more and more, and then start lifting off into the air. You should really be in a lotus position to do it – you can hurt yourself landing if you've got a dangling undercarriage.'

Many eastern holy men claim powers of levitation and though there is some obvious trickery – boys at the roadside in India 'levitate' for tourists, as western magicians might saw a woman in half – other levitations would seem to be genuine.

John Keel in his book *Jadoo* describes his meetings with holy men in India and Tibet in the 1950s. Many of them faked the evidence of their supposed powers but he was impressed by a Tibetan lama called Nyang-Pas who levitated for him; he simply stood up, put one hand on top of his stick as though to study himself, then rose up until he was sitting cross-legged in the air. There was no possibility of anything behind or below to help support him.

Some people have suggested that apparent levitations are nothing but collective hallucinations produced by hypnotic suggestion but that would hardly explain the photographs published by *The Illustrated London News* in 1936. They were taken in southern India while a *fakir* called Subbayah Pullavar levitated in front of 150 witnesses. Though the actual act of levitation took place inside a tent, which was then removed, he then remained horizontal in the air for four minutes, apparently in a trance. Several

*Levitation would seem to be impossible, but there are many who claim they can cancel the gravitational pull of the earth through meditation and mental discipline. Many photographs exist which apparently give incontrovertible proof that the pull of gravity can be defied. **Left**: Colin Evans at Wortley Hall, Finsbury Park on 27 November 1937. **Below**: A table levitating in Missouri, USA.*

Above: *Joseph of Copertino.* **Right:** *A pair of scissors levitated by a medium using her powers.*

his chair. Physicist Sir William Crookes, after carrying out extensive investigations, concluded that his powers were genuine. On one occasion he saw Home 'slowly rise up with a continuous gliding movement and remain about six inches off the ground for several seconds, when he slowly descended'. He was able to pass his hands under Home's feet and right round his body while he was in the air. Home could even extend his powers of levitation to other people and once Crookes' wife was lifted off the ground in her chair.

Home's description of his own levitation went like this: 'I feel no hands supporting me and, since the first time, I have never felt fear; though, should I have fallen from the ceiling of some rooms in which I have been raised, I could not have escaped serious injury. I am generally lifted up perpendicularly; my arms frequently become rigid and are drawn above my head, as though I were grasping the unseen power which slowly raises me from the floor.'

Home's most famous levitation was when, watched by three reputable witnesses – Lord Adare, the Master of Lindsay and Captain Wynne – he floated out of the window of a London house, 24 m (80 ft) from the ground, and back in at another.

Researchers have done their best to disprove the feat, suggesting that, with careful preparation, he might have rigged a rope to hang on to, while balancing on a narrow ledge between the window balconies. They point out that the witnesses were told to keep their seats and not to watch what happened through the window, which could indicate some form of trickery; it could be, however, that Home simply wanted to make sure that there was no chance of his re-entry being blocked, in case his powers waned suddenly.

The fact remains that in 40 years, during which his levitations were witnessed by such eminent people as the Emperor Napoleon III, Mark Twain, Ruskin and Thackeray, in all sorts of different venues, he was never once detected in a fraud.

Eventually Crookes, later to become President of the British Association for the Advancement of Science, wrote: 'The phenomena I am prepared to attest are so extraordinary ... that there is an antagonism in my mind between *reason*, which pronounces it to be scientifically impossible, and the consciousness that my senses, both of touch and sight, are not lying witnesses.'

witnesses tested the area all around for any apparatus that might be invisible to the naked eye but his only support was one hand resting lightly on a cloth-covered stick. After the performance, his supporters had to massage his limbs for several minutes before his joints were supple enough to bend.

Daniel Dunglas Home

Many mediums have apparently been able to levitate, but they have never managed to reproduce their feats under conditions that satisfy parapsychologists.

The most famous was Daniel Dunglas Home, the Victorian medium who produced many spectacular manifestations at seances. He frequently floated up to the ceiling, sometimes while still sitting in

Stigmata
SPONTANEOUS BLEEDING

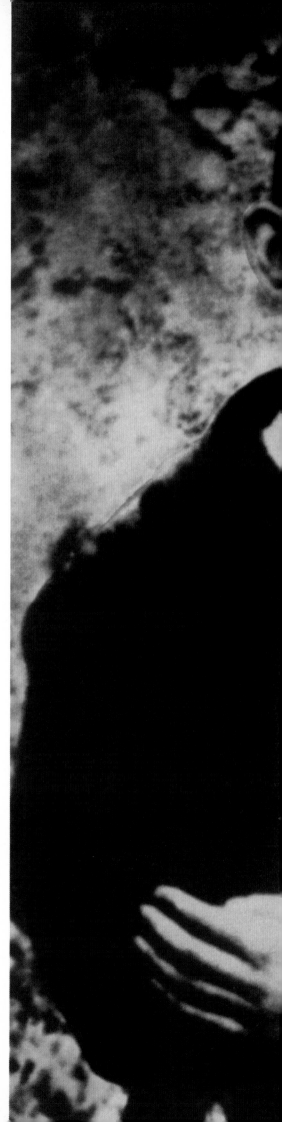

Padre Pio, a Capuchin monk, was praying alone in the chapel of his monastery when his fellow monks heard a sudden cry and found him lying unconscious with blood pouring from his hands, feet and his left side.

That was on 20 September 1918 and from that day until his death in 1968, the wounds, all on the traditional sites of the wounds suffered by Christ on the cross, bled continuously. Over the years he was examined by many doctors who found that the wounds went right through his hands, though there was no sign of inflammation at the edges.

Though he was forbidden to leave the monastery or write of his experiences and he always did his best to conceal his wounds when he said mass, word of what had happened spread and pilgrims flocked to the obscure Italian town in the hope of seeing the miracle for themselves.

Female Stigmatics
Another of the 20th century's most famous stigmatics was Teresa Neumann, a Bavarian peasant woman who suffered from a mysterious illness that left her blind and paralyzed. She was cured after a vision of St Theresa of Lisieux and, quite suddenly, the stigmata appeared. For 32 years the bleeding – from her hands and feet, her side and her forehead – began on Fridays. Over the weekend she would often lose as much as 0.5 litres (1 pt) of blood, then on Sunday she would return to normal.

*Above: Teresa Neumann weeping tears of blood. She would bleed from Friday to Sunday, losing much blood in the process. **Right:** Padre Pio, with the signs of the stigmata showing on his hands.*

Many stigmatics have undergone extensive tests which rule out any possibility of fraud. Louise Lateau, a peasant girl who bled regularly from the hands every Friday, was examined by experts at the Belgian Academy. One of their tests was to seal one of her hands into a glass globe. The blood flowed just as before, though in her case there was no apparent wound. When it stopped, it left no sign but a slight reddening of the skin.

The majority of stigmatics are women; they often come from poor backgrounds and are deeply religious. Many have a history of unexplained illnesses, probably psychosomatic in origin. Doctors, well aware that the mind can produce dramatic physical symptoms, believe that stigmata are the products of hysteria. This, they hasten to explain, does not mean that the subjects are over-excitable or uncontrolled, but only that they are experiencing a state of emotion so extreme that it produces physical signs.

Many stigmatics only bleed on Fridays, the day of the Crucifixion, or only at major religious festivals such as Easter or Lent and it is noticeable that the wounds occur on the places of the body associated with Christ's wounds in religious paintings and church statues. In fact, the Romans crucified their victims by tying their arms and driving nails through their wrists. The wounds on the palms of stigmatics appear there because that is where they *believe* that the nails were placed.

Cloretta Robinson

One recent case, reported in *General Psychiatry* in 1974, is remarkable because it involved a young American Baptist girl, not only the first black stigmatic but the first non-Catholic.

Cloretta Robinson was a devout 10-year-old who spent many hours a day praying and reading the Bible. One day, in school, she opened her hands and saw blood pouring from them. She was taken to the doctor, who could find no wound when he wiped away the blood, but when it happened again she was referred to a specialist. Doctors looked on in amazement: bleeding would begin with a few drops oozing out of the centre of her palm, then, while they watched, the blood would stream out. Afterwards, only a slight pink mark was left.

The phenomenon was witnessed by teachers and children, nurses and doctors, scores of people in all. Psychiatrists who were called in to examine the girl could come up with only one explanation: psychologically induced bleeding.

Famous Disappearances

INTO THE UNKNOWN
THE MARY CELESTE

On 5 December 1872, the crew of the British sailing ship the *Dei Gratia*, sailing from New York to Gibraltar, sighted another ship, veering erratically from left to right.

As they drew nearer, Captain Morehouse could see no one at the wheel of the ship, no one on her deck. When he hailed her without raising a reply, he sent a party in a rowing boat to investigate.

A Ship with no Crew

They found the ship deserted. The lifeboat was missing, and so were the navigation instruments. Though she had suffered some storm damage, the ship was in no danger of sinking. One of the hatch covers was off and though there was some water in the hold, the pumps could have dealt with it quite easily. Down below, everything seemed orderly: in the crew's quarters dry clothes lay on the bunks, oilskins and boots were still there. The ship was the *Mary Celeste*.

The *Mary Celeste* had sailed for Genoa on 4 November with a cargo of crude alcohol. The master was Captain Benjamin Briggs, an upright, God-fearing man, well-liked by the seamen under his command. His wife and two-year-old daughter, Sophia, were with him on the voyage, as well as seven crew members.

The log book recorded that the weather for the first three weeks of the voyage had been good but that, once past the Azores, it had changed for the worse, with a moderate gale blowing. It was not serious enough to alarm an experienced sailor and on 24 November the Captain ordered some of the sails to be furled. On the morning of 25 November the log recorded the ship's bearings. That was the last entry.

Captain Morehouse detailed three members of his crew to sail the *Mary Celeste* back to Gibraltar, where a public inquiry was ordered and very many wild rumours circulated.

One of the first stories to be spread around was that Captain Briggs and Morehouse had plotted together to collect salvage money on the ship. A more blood-thirsty tale was that the crew of the *Dei Gratia*, imagining that the *Mary Celeste* carried valuable cargo, slaughtered everyone on board. There was no evidence for either theory and promising looking clues came to nothing. A sword was discovered under the captain's bed with what appeared to be bloodstains but turned out to be rust. Some of the casks of alcohol were dry, which led to speculation about a drunken rampage but, apart from the fact that commercial alcohol would have given the men severe pains long before they became drunk, there was no sign of any rampage on board.

The inquiry dragged on for three months without the puzzle being solved. The most likely explanation seemed to be that the crew had panicked in a storm, believing that the ship was sinking, and had taken to the lifeboat, only to be drowned in rough seas.

An Unlucky Ship

Many people still find it impossible to believe that Captain Briggs, an experienced sailor and a steady, intelligent man, would have rushed his wife and daughter into a tiny boat in the face of minor damage to the ship. They prefer more colourful explanations: the members of the crew were devoured by a sea-monster, abducted by a UFO or sucked up by a whirlwind. Another idea is that everyone on board was driven mad by contaminated food or water and, delirious, they threw themselves overboard. If that was so, then by happy chance they must have finished off all the dangerously contaminated foodstuff, as the crew from the *Dei Gratia*, who sailed the vessel back to Gibraltar, experienced no ill effects.

The *Mary Celeste* had been known as an unlucky ship even before Captain Briggs's ill-fated voyage. Afterwards she changed hands 17 times in 12 years until, in 1885, she was deliberately run aground in an insurance swindle.

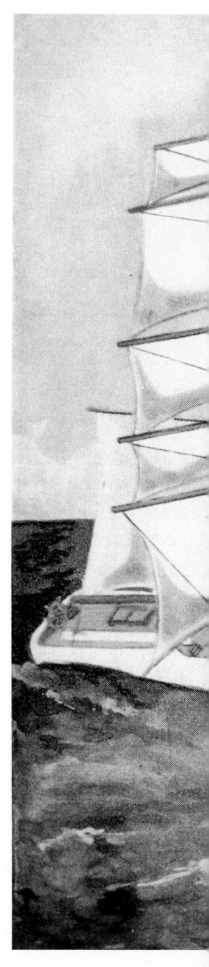

Benjamin Spooner Briggs, Master of the Mary Celeste, who vanished from the ship with his wife, two-year-old daughter and the entire crew.

GLENN MILLER

On a December afternoon in 1944 a single-engined aircraft set off from a Bedfordshire airfield, bound for Paris. It never arrived and its occupants, the pilot and two American officers, were never seen again. Their fate is a mystery that still intrigues music lovers, for one of the officers was the band leader Glenn Miller, famous for such hits as *String of Pearls*, *In the Mood*, *Pennsylvania 6500* and *Moonlight Serenade*.

When the Allied invasion of Europe was imminent, General Eisenhower considered that Major Glenn Miller's unique big-band sound was just what was needed to keep up the morale of the forces. In June 1944 Miller arrived in Britain with his 60-piece orchestra and began broadcasting as the American Band of the Allied Expeditionary Forces.

Towards the end of the year he was determined to give a full-scale concert in Paris and, although he had to contend with all sorts of obstacles, he insisted on going ahead himself to make the arrangements, though this would normally have been the job of the band's manager.

No News of the Band Leader

Two days after his departure, the orchestra arrived in Paris expecting Miller to meet them, only to find that no one had had any news of him. In spite of repeated searches both on sea and land, no trace of wreckage or bodies was ever found.

Glenn Miller and his 60-piece orchestra, known as the American Band of the Allied Expeditionary Forces.

The obvious explanation was that the aircraft, a Norwegian D-64, had come down in the Channel, the occupants trapped inside and drowned. When they set off it was foggy enough to ground all RAF training flights and though the experienced pilot was confident that he could get through, he might have lost his way and run out of fuel. Another possibility is that the wings of the plane iced up, so that it stalled and came down in the sea.

A Possible Cover-Up

These explanations have never stilled the rumours of a cover-up over the circumstances of Miller's disappearance and many fans refused to believe the official story. Some thought that he had been shot down by mistake by a British fighter, or that he had been so badly disfigured by the crash that he preferred to spend the rest of his life in solitude, or that he was a spy engaged in a secret mission that ended disastrously in France.

Former RAF pilot John Edwards spent more than 12 years trying to find the answer and decided that Miller was not aboard the Norseman when it crashed, having changed planes at another British airfield and arrived safely in Paris in a Dakota.

Edwards claims that Glenn Miller, who was a known womanizer, was murdered in Pigalle in Paris, an area full of prostitutes and criminals at that time. He died of a fractured skull but, because of the seedy circumstances, the authorities wanted to hush up the scandal. During his investigation he found that many pertinent reports had been destroyed and details such as the aircrew report were unaccountably vague:

But pieces of information I have collected over the years eventually all fell into place. I have evidence that an American military doctor in Paris signed Miller's death certificate. A retired US Air Force lieutenant-colonel recalls being told by the provost marshall's police office in Paris that Miller had been murdered. And I know a man in Miller's band who stated that it was common knowledge to those close to him that his boss was murdered in Paris.

There was an extra reason for fans to hope that, one day, the riddle would be solved, for when the band leader left England he had with him a case full of scores of new Glenn Miller numbers. Even now, they could still come to light.

AGATHA CHRISTIE

Agatha Christie has been celebrated as the queen of crime for more than half a century but when she died in 1976 she left behind, along with over 80 novels, a real-life mystery as puzzling as any she had ever invented.

On a bitterly cold December night in 1926, when she was 34, she left home with a few pounds in her purse, drove off into the night and disappeared for nearly two weeks.

'They Think I've Murdered My Wife'

Newspaper headlines screamed the news of her disappearance with many theories ranging from kidnapping to murder. Thousands of people joined police from four counties as they scoured the countryside. The Silent Pool was dredged, trained dogs were brought out. Most of the searchers were convinced that the famous writer had committed suicide and that it only remained to find the body.

Meanwhile the police kept a careful eye on her husband, Colonel Archibald Christie. 'They think I've murdered my wife,' he confided to an office colleague.

While the hysteria mounted, a young woman who registered as Teresa Neele was holidaying at the Hydro Hotel in Harrogate, Yorkshire. She went shopping in the town, played billiards, went for long walks and even danced the Charleston one evening. She told fellow guests that she was a visitor from South Africa.

The hotel manager, who had read the reports of Agatha Christie's disappearance, suspected that the missing writer and his guest were one and the same and informed the police. On 14 December Archie Christie arrived at the hotel and confronted his wife as she was about to go in to dinner. As he approached she told a group of her fellow guests calmly: 'Fancy, my brother has just arrived.'

His claim that she was suffering from loss of memory was backed by doctors but Agatha Christie was no amnesia victim. While in Harrogate she had written to Harrods in Knightsbridge, where she had mislaid a diamond ring, asking that if it was found, it should be returned to Mrs Neele at the Hydro Hotel.

*The disappearance of Agatha Christie, a 'real' happening, just as dramatic as any of her detective stories. **Below**: Police reconstructing the supposed accident to the runaway car at Newlands Corner.*

The press suspected an elaborate publicity stunt and there were demands that the Christies should repay the £3,000 cost of the police search. However, the novelist's popularity was too well-established to suffer permanently and the memory of the strange events of 1926 gradually faded. In years to come she would agree to interviews only on the understanding that the matter was not discussed. She was always a private, even secretive, person and in her autobiography she passed over the episode with vague hints about a nervous breakdown.

A Traumatic Time of Life

It happened at a most traumatic time of her life. Archie Christie had fallen in love with another woman – a Miss Nancy Neele – and asked Agatha to divorce him. On the morning of her departure they had quarrelled and Archie had packed his bags and gone to spend the weekend with Nancy.

The simple explanation could be that, angry and miserable, she needed time to herself to think things over but in that case she could easily have told the police the truth, before the great search was mounted, without agreeing to return home. More likely, she wanted to stage a disappearance to embarrass her husband, even to punish him by drawing public attention to his behaviour. As a mystery writer, she knew perfectly well that, until she was found, he was likely to come under police suspicion and that might have been a welcomed thought for a hurt, rejected wife. On the other hand, it could have been a ploy to win him back – perhaps she hoped that he would be overcome by worry and remorse and realize that he still loved her after all. Whatever the explanation, her use of the name Neele was obviously no accident.

Agatha Christie as she was in later life. In her autobiography she hinted of a nervous breakdown to account for her disappearance.

EVA PERON

When Eva Peron died in 1952, her body was embalmed at a cost of $100,000 and there were plans to build memorials throughout Argentina in honour of the charismatic woman who had been adored and revered. But the plans were never put into effect; instead, Eva's body disappeared, to remain in mysterious exile for 16 years, while the poor of Argentina went on grieving for her and the slogans on the walls of Buenos Aires demanded 'Give back the body of Evita' – the 'little Eva' they loved.

Eva was born into poverty and was an illegitimate child. By the age of 15 she had moved to Buenos Aires with her first lover, her heart set on an acting career. She was working for a radio station when she met and captivated Colonel Juan Peron, who was twice her age. By the time he had become president she was his wife.

Argentina's Idol

Evita appeared in public swathed in costly mink as she organized programmes to aid the poor and diamonds flashed on her hands as she threw the crowd toys for their children. No one seemed to see the irony: the people of Argentina saw no wrong in her and when she died of cancer at the age of 33 the nation was plunged into mourning. When her body lay in state two million people filed past her coffin.

Before a permanent resting place for Eva's body had been decided upon, Peron was ousted from power and exiled to Spain while Argentina's new military rulers did their best to discredit the Perons. They displayed the former president's lavish homes, custom-built sports cars, safes bulging with money and Eva's fabulous jewels. In spite of all this, the cult of Eva worship grew and the new leaders feared that her embalmed body might become a rallying point for those aiming to reinstate Peron.

The Body Vanishes

In December 1955 Eva's body vanished, spirited away at night by the army's intelligence service. Once the news of the body snatching leaked out, Peron supporters ran riot; the more the military

leaders tried to stifle the outcry, the louder it became. The theft remained a major source of grievance for the next 16 years, while the whereabouts of the corpse remained a mystery.

Much of what followed is unclear; what is known is that the new leaders of Argentina stopped short of having the body destroyed and instead decided to hide it. It was sealed in a packing case and moved from one hiding place to another over the next few months, before being shipped to Europe where it was stored in the cellar of the Argentina ambassador in Bonn.

In the autumn of 1956 the body was placed in a coffin, supposedly that of an Italian widow, and moved to Milan. It was buried under the name of Maria Maggi de Magistris in the Mussocco cemetery where it remained for 15 years, its whereabouts known only to a select few.

The Body is Returned

During those years, a succession of military juntas wrestled with the economic problems of Argentina. Eventually the head of one junta, Lieutenant-General Alexjandro Lanusse, decided to invite Peron to return to Argentina and, as a first act of good faith, he arranged for Eva's body to be returned to him.

When Peron saw the face of his long-dead wife, looking as tranquil and lovely as she had looked in life, he burst into tears, saying: 'She is not dead; she is only sleeping.'

In 1972 Peron at last returned to his homeland and a year later he was elected president with his second wife, Isabel, as vice-president. His rule was cut short by his death on 1 July 1974 and, as he lay in state, Eva lay beside him.

Once Peron was buried, Eva's body went into storage again. It was not until October 1976 that the nation's leaders agreed on a permanent burial place. Eva, still beautiful with her blonde hair, her skin almost translucent, was finally laid to rest in an underground family vault in a cemetery in Buenos Aires. The tomb was built to be as secure as a bank vault, to ensure that no one could ever steal the body of Eva Peron again.

The photo on the right gives a good indication of the glamour, smile and style of Eva Peron, who captivated the people of Argentina. They are still mourning her death even now, 40 years later.

CHAPTER THREE

UNSOLVED CRIMES

◆

The most fascinating crime stories are those that remain unsolved to intrigue and puzzle future generations. While novelists can provide neat endings with all the clues explained and the loose ends tied, real life crime can be far more baffling, with contradictory evidence, misleading statements and unanswered questions. Murderers walk free, the innocent become prime suspects and crime historians are left to sift the facts and produce ingenious and sometimes bizarre new answers.

Lord Lucan

THE VANISHING PEER

A distraught young woman wearing only a blood-stained nightdress burst through the doors of the Plumber's Arms in Belgravia, London on a night in early November 1974, sobbing: 'Help me, help me, I've just escaped from a murderer.'

The 26-year-old Countess of Lucan had fled from her home at 46 Lower Belgrave Street, where police were to find the body of her children's nanny, Sandra Rivett, stuffed inside a canvas mailbag. Nearby was a length of blood-stained lead piping, bound in surgical tape.

Lady Lucan told police that she had spending a quiet evening at home with her three children and their nanny, Sandra. Though Thursday was Sandra's evening off she had changed her plans and stayed at home. Lady Lucan normally made a cup of tea at 9 o'clock but that evening Sandra offered to make it instead. When she failed to re-appear, Lady Lucan went down to the basement kitchen to investigate and claimed that in the darkness her husband had attacked and beaten her. He told her that Sandra was dead and that her body was in the basement. They both went upstairs and when he went to fetch a towel to clean up her wounds, Lady Lucan saw her chance for escape and ran from the house.

A Terrible Catastrophe

By the time police arrived at the house, Lord Lucan had disappeared into the night. About three-quarters of an hour later his mother arrived, saying that he had phoned her to say there had been a 'terrible catastrophe'.

Two hours after the murder Lucan arrived at the home of an old friend, Susan Maxwell-Scott, in Sussex. While there, he wrote to a friend, Bill Shand Kydd, saying:

> The circumstantial evidence against me is strong in that V will say it was all my doing and I will lie doggo for a while, but I am only concerned about the children ...
>
> V has demonstrated her hatred for me in the past and would do anything to see me accused.

When he left Mrs Maxwell-Scott's home in the early hours of the morning, Lucan said he was going back 'to clear things up'. In fact, he never went back, or phoned the police to give his side of the story. The car he had been using, borrowed from a friend, was abandoned the day after the murder in Newhaven, Sussex, a port with a regular ferry service to France.

A Possible Motive

Police investigations failed to uncover any evidence that another man had been present in the house that night. The Lucans had separated in 1973 after an unhappy marriage, in which the 39-year-old Earl, an unsuccessful professional gambler, had lost all his money and piled up large debts. The police reckon that he hatched the murder plot to dispose of his wife and regain custody of the children. Knowing that Thursday was the nanny's night off, he let himself into the house, removed the light bulb from the basement stairs and waited in the darkness for his wife. He killed the nanny by mistake, then tried to batter his wife.

He then vanished without trace, without touching any of his bank accounts. At first police suspected that wealthy friends might be shielding Lucan but their search through the ranks of his friends and associates yielded no clues to his whereabouts.

The inquest on Sandra Rivett's death took place seven months later and the jury not only recorded her death as murder but named Lord Lucan as the murderer. The extraordinary result of this inquest is that, as far as the public is concerned, Lucan has been convicted of murder without ever having been tried or convicted under normal criminal procedure. As a direct result of this case the law was changed by the Criminal Law Act of 1977 so that this event could never happen again.

A Contract Killing?

In his book *Trail of Havoc: In the Steps of Lord Lucan*, Patrick Marnham argues that John Lucan did not murder Sandra Rivett or attack Lady Lucan but that he hired a contract killer to do the job, letting him into the house before leaving to establish his own alibi.

Evidence was given that Lucan phoned

WANTED FOR MURDER

LORD LUCAN

to book a table at his club at about 8.30 in the evening and that about 8.45 he was seen on the doorstep of the club. Marnham argues that, if Lucan planned to kill his wife when she made the tea at her usual time of around 9 o'clock, after removing the basement light and concealing himself, he would surely have made sure of arriving at the house by 8 o'clock, and that it would have taken him at least 10 minutes to get from the club to the house.

Marnham believes that Lucan, having established his alibi, planned to arrive in time to remove the body but instead walked in on the scene of a botched job. As the killer fled and Lady Lucan screamed, it was her husband's voice she heard trying to keep her quiet, his hand across her mouth to silence her, and she assumed that he was the attacker.

Marnham draws attention to a number of puzzling features. For instance, when blue-grey wool fibres, supposedly from Lord Lucan's trousers, were found in the basement, on the murder weapon, on a washbasin, bath-towel and in the abandoned car, why were none found on the mailbag, into which the murderer had packed the doubled up body?

Lucan's Disappearance

Unless Lord Lucan is found alive, we shall never know all the answers. Despite all the supposed sightings and police searches that have spread from Africa to America, there have been no traces of him; seven years after the murder he was declared legally dead.

Superintendent Dave Gerring, who was involved in the investigation, is among those who find the suicide idea hard to accept. He said: 'Lucan is still hiding somewhere and he is the only man who knows the full story. He is a lord and a gentleman but he is still a gambler and he is gambling on the odds that no one will ever find him.'

Lizzie Borden

AND THE AXE MURDERS

Lizzie Borden took an axe
And gave her mother 40 whacks.
When she saw what she had done
Gave her father 41.

That cruel jingle was to follow Lizzie Borden to the grave, over 40 years after she had been acquitted of murdering her parents.

On the morning of 4 August 1892, the maid, Bridget Sullivan, heard Lizzie calling in alarm: 'Come down quick. Father's dead; somebody came in and killed him.' Andrew Borden lay dead in the living room of his home in Fall River, Massachusetts, his head and face hacked to an unrecognizable pulp. He was lying on the sofa, where he often took a nap and there was no sign of resistance. The doctor who examined the body believed that he had been killed by the first of ten blows and that he had been dead for only 20 minutes.

There was a second shock to come. Abby Borden, Andrew's second wife, had planned to visit a sick friend that morning but she never left the house and

her body was later discovered on the floor of the spare bedroom. Like her husband, she had been savagely hacked to death and had died 90 minutes before him.

Those who maintained that the murderer came from outside the household pointed out that the first policeman on the scene did not search the house and left no guard behind. Even so, it seems unlikely that the killer could have committed two murders, 90 minutes apart, without attracting the attention of either Lizzie or Bridget, then escaped in broad daylight along a busy street, managing to take the bloody murder weapon with him, or to dispose of it before he left.

Besides the murdered couple, there were four people living in the house at the time but Emma, Lizzie's elder sister, was out of town visiting friends. Suspicion might have fallen heavily on John Morse, Mrs Borden's brother, who had arrived unexpectedly the day before but he had been visiting another relative at the time and his alibi was unshakeable. Only Bridget and Lizzie were at home at the time and the police never found any reason to suspect Bridget.

Possible Motives

The net closed inexorably around Lizzie, who told police that she had been in the barn looking for fish-hook sinkers when the murders took place. Though she was a quiet spinster who taught in Sunday school and was active in charitable causes, she was known to dislike her step-mother and there were long-standing grievances about money with her dour and unbending father.

She was charged with murder and brought to trial in June 1893, but the circumstantial evidence against her proved too flimsy and she was found not guilty. Two points counted heavily in her favour. The first was that the murder weapon was never identified for certain and Lizzie would have had no opportunity to get rid of it. The second was the evidence given by those who had seen Lizzie only a few minutes after the second murder was committed, who said that there had been no sign of bloodstains on her clothes or her person.

Lizzie returned to the bleak old house to live with her sister until they parted company in 1923. She never married and in later years she lived alone, always followed by rumours and taunts about her supposed crime.

Victoria Lincoln, a writer from Fall River, in her book *A Private Disgrace*, suggested that Lizzie suffered from bouts of psychomotor epilepsy, a rare condition

kept secret even within the family, resulting in short spells of violent insanity after which she would have no memory of her actions. However, that theory provides no convincing explanation for the lack of bloodstains after such a gory crime.

Another Explanation

In 1971 journalist Edward Radin made out a good case for accusing the maid Bridget Sullivan of the murder. On that sweltering day, when everyone in the house knew that she was feeling unwell, Mrs Borden had told her to clean the windows. Perhaps she gave another order later which turned the girl's resentment into a murderous rage – but then why should she turn on the sleeping Mr Borden?

Only Lizzie (and perhaps one other person) knew the truth, so the full story will never be known.

Left: Andrew Borden was hacked to death in the sitting room of his home in Fall River, Massachusetts.
***Below**: A sketch of Lizzie's trial in June 1893 shows her with her counsel, ex-Governor Robinson.*

Roberto Calvi

THE POPE'S BANKER

Early on the morning of 18 June 1982, the body of a man was seen swinging from scaffolding below Blackfriars Bridge in London. When police cut down the corpse, they found his pockets bulging with over £7,000 in foreign banknotes and several large stones.

In their efforts to discover his identity, the London authorities contacted police in Rome and back came the answer: 'You've got our banker.' The banker in question was Roberto Calvi, chairman of the influential Banco Ambrosiano, which had for many years enjoyed such a close relationship with the Vatican that Calvi was nicknamed 'the Pope's banker'.

Calvi was in deep trouble when he had fled, six days earlier, from his apartment in Rome. He had been found guilty of illegal currency dealing and sentenced to four years in gaol. For some time there had been grave suspicions about the workings of the Ambrosiano bank and Calvi knew only too well that any detailed investigation would reveal the enormous financial labyrinth of fraud that he had built up.

In the week after his disappearance, Ambrosiano began its headlong tumble into bankruptcy. For years Calvi had been passing shares between mysterious Panamanian and Liechtenstein companies at vastly inflated prices and raising huge loans on those fictitious prices. Hundreds of thousands of dollars had disappeared, the companies turned out to exist only in name and their ownership was traced back to the Vatican bank.

The First Inquest

The disgrace and ruin that awaited Calvi seemed to provide a sound motive for suicide; there was no hard evidence of foul play and no marks of violence on the body. When the inquest was held five weeks later the jury returned a verdict of suicide.

The Calvi family, who had been in touch with the banker while he was in hiding with his bodyguard in a London flat, was outraged. They staged an all-out campaign to show that his death was not suicide but murder.

The family found it impossible to believe that a stout, 62-year-old man who suffered from vertigo would choose a method of suicide which involved climbing over a parapet and across scaffolding, all the time weighed down by pockets full of stones, when he had enough barbiturates in his lodgings to do the job quietly and painlessly. In interviews before he left Rome, Calvi had hinted at fears for his safety. He had told his family that he would reveal all at the appeal hearing, which was to have taken place four days after his death. Calvi's wife, Clara, suspected that factions in the Vatican, engaged in their own internal power struggle and incensed by Ambrosiano's involvement in international politics through its financial dealings, were behind the murder. Calvi claimed to have channelled $50 million to the Solidarity movement in Poland, and some may have felt this was a threat to the carefully cultivated relationship between the Vatican and the communist world.

The scene on the River Thames, under Blackfriars Bridge, where the body of Roberto Calvi was found hanging from scaffolding. Suicide seemed the obvious explanation but Calvi's family have always believed that he was murdered.

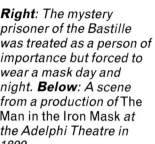

Right: The mystery prisoner of the Bastille was treated as a person of importance but forced to wear a mask day and night. **Below**: A scene from a production of The Man in the Iron Mask at the Adelphi Theatre in 1899.

The Man in the Iron Mask

AN UNSOLVED MYSTERY

He became one of the most enigmatic figures in history, the prisoner whose face was never seen, whose name was never spoken, whose crime was never known. To the world, he became The Man in the Iron Mask.

While he was imprisoned in the Bastille in 17th century France, rumours about him spread swiftly throughout the world. It was said that he was a royal bastard, so closely resembling the King, Louis XIV, that his face must never be seen. Some went even further, claiming that Louis was the bastard and that the masked prisoner was the rightful King.

Certainly, it was on Louis XIV's personal order that the prisoner should remain masked throughout his 34-year incarceration. If he attempted to remove the mask, so much as hinted at his identity, or tried to talk about anything beyond the immediate necessities of his daily life, his gaolers had orders to kill him immediately. His name did not appear in the prison records and was never used either to his face or in letters about him. He was usually referred to as 'the prisoner you sent me' or, as he grew older, 'the ancient prisoner'.

In all other ways, he was treated as an important person and the King and his ministers regularly asked about his welfare. His room was well furnished, his clothes expensive and he was allowed to practise his religion freely.

The Prisoner's Death

With his death in November 1703 the mystery only intensified, with extraordinary steps taken to ensure that his identity remained a secret for ever. Every item of furniture and equipment he had used was burned or destroyed, all his clothes thrown into a furnace, the walls of his cell were scraped and scoured and the floor tiles removed, in case he had attempted to leave behind any message.

Even the King's successors were not allowed to share the secret; Louis XVI searched the royal archives in vain, trying to discover the prisoner's identity to satisfy the curiosity of his wife, Marie Antoinette.

The first written references to the prisoner came when the journals of Etienne du Jonca, the King's Lieutenant at the Bastille, were published in 1761. He recorded the arrival of a masked man 'whose name is not mentioned', who was transferred to the Bastille from another prison on 18 September 1698 and his death five years later, saying that he was buried on 20 November in the graveyard of St Paul under the false name of Marchioly. Du Jonca says that the mask was made of black velvet; other sources describe it as being made of iron reinforced with steel, fitted with a chin piece of steel springs to allow the prisoner to eat and drink.

Eustache Dauger

The first clues to the prisoner's identity came with the French Revolution. In the archives was a message from the Minister of War to M. de Saint Mars, the governor who had charge of the prisoner all along, relaying the King's command to take charge of a man named Eustache Dauger. The message, dated July 1669, the year the masked man was first imprisoned, read:

> It is of the utmost importance that he should be most closely guarded and that he should in no way give information about himself nor send letters to anyone at all. You will yourself once a day have to take enough food for the day to this wretch and you must on no account listen for any reason at all to what he may want to say to you, always threatening to kill him if he opens his mouth to speak of anything but his necessities.

Letters from the King himself saying that Eustache Dauger must be kept strictly incommunicado were also found, together with papers giving details of Dauger's imprisonment which correspond exactly with what is known of the imprisonment of the masked man.

Even then, Dauger's identity was obscure but patient research eventually discovered a lieutenant of the King's Guards by that name; a man who seems to have disappeared after 1668 and whose death was never recorded. His brother was close to the King but Eustache was often in trouble and seems to have been involved in court intrigue, perhaps even with the Satanism and black masses encouraged by the King's mistress, Madame de Montespan. But exactly what crimes he committed against the King or why it was so essential that his face should not be seen has never been explained; we can only go on guessing.

The Bravo Case

A DOSE OF TARTAR EMETIC

Charles Bravo, who died on 21 April 1876, was poisoned. That much has been clearly established; apart from that, however, the facts of the case remain a mystery.

The Bravos, Charles and Florence, lived in an imposing mansion in a south London suburb. Their marriage, which had started out very happily, began to have its problems. Charles was arrogant and sometimes violent; Florence, who was a little too fond of alcohol, was not strong and had just suffered the second of two miscarriages.

She had been married before, to a drunkard and womanizer and, after her first husband's death, had turned to an older man for comfort and had an affair with a 62-year-old doctor named Gully. Later, Florence and her companion, Mrs Jane Cox, maintained that Charles became wildly jealous after the marriage and was always venting his rage over the affair.

Suddenly Sick

On the evening of 18 April 1876 Florence, still recovering from her miscarriage, went to bed early and Mrs Cox went to sit with her. Soon after Charles went up to the spare bedroom he was occupying at the time, a maid heard him calling desperately for hot water – though Mrs Cox, in the next room, claimed to have heard nothing.

The maid and Mrs Cox found Charles vomiting out of the window and obviously very ill indeed. Several doctors were summoned and they did their best to find out if Charles had taken anything that could account for the symptoms. He maintained that he had taken nothing but laudanum for toothache.

Charles Bravo died after three days of painful illness, still maintaining that he had taken nothing; however, it was found that he had died from a large dose of a tartar emetic. The inquest, run by a coroner who was obviously convinced that it was suicide, brought in an open verdict but so much criticism followed the sketchy inquiry that a second inquest was opened lasting 23 days.

Throughout, Mrs Cox maintained that Charles had committed suicide because of his uncontrollable jealousy. His last message to her now came out as: 'I have taken poison for Gully.'

The origin of the poison was never discovered but, though no tartar emetic was found in the house, it had been used in the stables to doctor the horses a few months before. This time the verdict was 'wilful murder' but no names were cited.

Right: A sketch of the court proceedings at the Bravo inquest showing Mrs Cox facing cross examination. *Far right*: The Bravo poisoning case excited great interest in the press.

PRICE THREEPENCE.

THE PICTORIAL WORLD

AN ILLUSTRATED WEEKLY NEWSPAPER

No. 128. Vol. V. {Registered at the General Post Office as a Newspaper.}   SATURDAY, AUGUST 12th, 1876.   **THREEPENCE.** Per Post, 3½d.

THE PRIORY

Mrs CHAs BRAVO.

EXAMINATION OF MRS CHAs BRAVO

MRS. COX

DR. GULLY

THE LATE MR. CHAs D.T. BRAVO. BARRISTER-AT-LAW

THE "BALHAM MYSTERY": PORTRAITS OF THE LATE MR. BRAVO, MRS. C. BRAVO, MRS. COX, AND DR. GULLY

Jack the Ripper

AN EVIL MONSTER

Even now, a century after Jack the Ripper's three-month reign of terror in London's East End, the very name chills to the marrow. The killer came from the darkness to strike down his victims in the most brutal, bestial way.

The Ripper murdered at least five women, though some criminologists believe the true number to be eleven. To this day, all that is known for certain is that the Ripper was left-handed and, according to the police surgeons, had some medical knowledge. Witnesses who glimpsed someone hurrying from the scene of several of the crimes described a tall, slim, pale man with a black moustache whose walk was young and vigorous.

Pretty Polly

The grim series of murders began on 31 August, 1888. Mary Ann Nicholls, known as Pretty Polly, was trying to earn fourpence, the price of a doss-house bed, confident of success because she was wearing her new straw bonnet. In the early hours of the morning a policeman discovered her body lying in the gutter. Her throat was cut and her body slashed open from throat to stomach.

The murder of a prostitute was, in itself, nothing unusual in the days when the sleazy drinking dens around the docks were packed with foreign seamen and women were forced by poverty to sell their bodies, but the bloody ferocity of the killing marked it out.

Dark Annie

The murderer struck again a week later, killing 'Dark Annie' Chapman who was 47 and dying of tuberculosis. Annie's body was found by a porter from Spitalfields Market, in a quiet yard often used by prostitutes and their clients, and once more the corpse was savagely gutted with some of the organs removed, along with two of her front teeth.

Soon after Annie's death, the Central News Agency in Fleet Street received a letter that read: 'I keep on hearing that the police have caught me. But they won't fix me yet . . . I am down on certain types of women and I won't stop ripping them until I get buckled.

'Grand job, that last job was. I gave the lady no time to squeal. I love my work and want to start again. You will soon hear from me, with my funny little game . . . Next time I shall clip the ears off and send them to the police just for jolly.'

The letter was signed Jack the Ripper. For the first time the mystery killer had a name.

Long Liz

On 30 September the steward of a Working Men's Club was driving his pony and cart into the club yard when the pony baulked at something lying in its path. Dismounting, he found himself bending over the body of Elizabeth 'Long Liz' Stride. Her throat had been cut and one of her ears slightly torn, but she had not been mutilated and the body was still warm. The Ripper had obviously been interrupted in the middle of his grisly work.

Frustrated blood lust was to lead the murderer to kill again that night. While police surgeons were examining the first

Above: *A contemporary illustration showing in vivid detail the discovery of a victim of Jack the Ripper.*

THE ILLUSTRATED POLICE NEWS
LAW COURTS AND WEEKLY RECORD

SATURDAY, OCTOBER 20, 1888.

INCIDENTS RELATING TO THE EAST END MURDERS

Price One Penny.

TRIAL OF BLOODHOUNDS

SIR C. WARREN VIEWING HANDWRITING ON WALL

LAST VICTIMS OF THE MYSTERIOUS MONSTER OF THE EAST-END

"LONG LIZ" AND HER FRIEND "ONE ARMED LIZ"

THE MYTRE SQUARE VICTIM. SHOWING WOUNDS ON FACE AND NECK

GOOD MORNING OLD COCK

FOUND DRUNK IN THE STREETS

IN A CELL SINGING A SONG HER LAST HOUR!

SKETCH OF SUPPOSED MURDERER

THE MAN SEEN HAUNTING HOUSE OF MR LUSK

ANOTHER SKETCH OF SUPPOSED MURDERER

THE MAN SEEN WITH LAST TWO VICTIMS.

LAST SCENE IN KATE EDDOWES LIFE

MITRE SQUARE

KELLY PARTS WITH KATE EDDOWES AND NEVER SEES HER ALIVE AGAIN

AT THE CORNER OF HOUNDS DITCH

The Jews are not the men that will be Blamed for Nothing

THE ASSASSIN DISTURBED AT HIS BLOODTHIRSTY WORK IN BERNER ST

83

THE DISCOVERY IN BERNER STREET

THE DISCOVERY IN MITRE SQUARE

LONDON'S REIGN OF TERROR: SCENES OF SUNDAY MORNING'S MURDERS IN THE EAST-END.

body, a constable discovered the mutilated body of Catherine Eddowes, her throat cut, some of her organs removed, her face slashed and her right earlobe partly severed.

A trail of blood led to a chalked message on a wall: 'The Jewes are not men to be blamed for nothing.' It could have been an important clue but Sir Charles Warren, head of the Metropolitan Police, was so worried about a possible outbreak of anti-semitic violence that he had it removed and kept secret.

After the double murder, hysteria swept London. Rumours about the Ripper's identity ran riot: he was a foreign seaman, a mad doctor, a Jewish butcher, a crazy midwife who hated prostitutes.

Mary Kelly

When five weeks passed without another Ripper crime, hopes rose that he was satiated at last. Then, on 9 November, Thomas Bowyer called to collect overdue rent from Mary Kelly. When he got no reply to his knocking he pushed aside the sacking curtain at the window and peered in. What he saw drove all thought of rent from his head and sent him running for help. Not only had Mary's throat been cut and her face savaged almost beyond recognition but parts of her body were arranged all around the room.

One of the last people to see Mary alive was George Hutchinson, an out-of-work night watchman. She had asked him for money to pay her rent and, when he said he could not help, had approached a man Hutchinson described as being about 35, with a pale complexion and dark eyes, wearing a long dark coat trimmed with astrakhan and walking very briskly.

With Mary Kelly's death, the horrific crimes ended as suddenly as they had began but speculation on the murderer's identity has continued ever since.

Two criminals confessed to being the Ripper. One was a Polish barber's assistant who had once trained as a surgeon and was charged with poisoning one woman and suspected of killing at least two others. When arrested he told the police 'You've got the Ripper at last.' The second was the poisoner of four London prostitutes who cried out, at the moment of his execution, 'I am Jack the ...' But there was never any concrete evidence to incriminate either man.

Some Different Explanations

Since then there have been many different solutions to the puzzle of the Ripper's identity. Inspector Robert Sagar, who had been on the case, said in his memoirs: 'We had good reason to suspect a man who lived in Butcher's Row, Aldgate. We watched him carefully. There was no doubt that the man was insane and, after a time, his friends thought it advisable to have him removed to a private asylum. After he was removed, there were no more Ripper atrocities.'

One of the wildest theories named Queen Victoria's eldest grandson, Prince Albert Victor, Duke of Clarence as a suspect, despite the fact that he was in Scotland on a shooting expedition at the time of the first two murders.

Writer Leonard Matters picked a surgeon called Dr Stanley as the prime suspect. He told a fascinating story about Stanley's son, who caught syphilis from Mary Kelly and died two years later, causing Stanley to hunt down the woman responsible, questioning and killing other street women along the way. Unfortunately there were few facts to back up the tale: it would be extraordinary for syphilis to kill within such a short time and the post mortem on Mary Kelly did not show that she was infected.

Writers, psychologists and detectives of every nation have been caught up in the fascination of the Ripper mystery. In 1992 the secret Scotland Yard files on the case will be finally made public but they are expected to cast little new light on the riddle.

Above: A satirical illustration which appeared in Punch in 1888 on the general incompetence of the police who were unable to catch the Ripper.

Spring-Heeled Jack
THE FLYING FIEND

Spring-heeled Jack was the nickname given to a mysterious fiend able to leap over high walls and roofs with superhuman ease, who pounced on his terrified victims with eyes glowing like hot coals, hands like claws of ice and a mouth spitting flames.

Tales of this devil-like attacker came first from those who had seen him leaping across Barnes Common, in south-west London in the 1830s. Then Polly Adams, a farmer's daughter who worked in a south London pub, was savagely attacked while walking across Blackheath by a strange creature who eventually fled, with amazing leaps through the air. Another woman, assaulted in a Clapham churchyard, gave a similar description of her assailant but at the beginning such accounts were dismissed as imagination or plain hysteria.

Then, in January 1838, the reports received official recognition when the Lord Mayor, Sir John Cowan, drew the public's attention to a letter from a terrified resident of Peckham, giving convincing details of the creature's exploits. Immediately, accounts flooded in from people who had been too scared or embarrassed to speak out before.

In February 1838, Jane Alsop answered a loud knocking on the door of her home in Bow to find a towering, cloaked figure standing on the step. As she raised her candle towards his shadowy face he grabbed her by the neck, pinning her head under his arm. As he ripped her dress and pawed at her body, she managed to tear herself away, screaming at the top of her voice. He grabbed her by her long hair, only letting go and making off into the darkness when her father and sisters ran to help her. Jane later told the police that he had been wearing something that looked like a close-fitting helmet on his head and a tight white costume under a black cloak. 'His face was hideous. His eyes were like balls of fire and he vomited blue and white flames. His hands were like claws, but icy cold.'

Lucy Scales and her sister were leaving their brother's house when a cloaked figure leaped out at them in Green Dragon Alley, Limehouse, spitting flames that temporarily blinded them. Their brother heard their cries and found them lying dazed on the cobbles, with a giant figure towering over them. The attacker ran, bounding easily over a brick wall, more than twice the height of a man.

Panic spread rapidly, with newspapers labelling Jack as 'public enemy number one' and demanding immediate action. Sightings spread from London to the Home Counties but the descriptions of the creature were so fantastic that the police were at a loss; none of their usual procedures helped in the search for such a monster. Vigilante squads were formed and rewards offered. Even the Duke of Wellington, then nearly 70, rode out on horseback in an attempt to hunt it down.

The last account of this fiendish creature came as late as 1904, when people in the Everton area of Liverpool chased him as he bounded from roof to roof, eventually leaping effortlessly over a row of terraced houses and disappearing into the distance – never to be seen again. Perhaps, after all, Jack was only an athletic villain who enjoyed frightening his victims, whose fevered imaginations embroidered the story.

In these two illustrations taken from 'Penny Dreadfuls' of the time, 'Spring-heeled Jacks' are depicted flying over chimney tops and gates.

CHAPTER FOUR

STRANGE CREATURES

◆

If nature can produce such oddities as a man with two bodies, or a child mothered by a wolf, she probably has plenty of surprises still in store. If only a few of the stories told by explorers and travellers are true, unidentified monsters still lurk in the depths of the ocean and man's distant ancestors still roam the unexplored regions of the high mountains. Past generations have believed firmly in vampires and werewolves and though it may be comforting to dismiss such beliefs as mere superstition, study of the evidence makes it difficult to distinguish reality from fantasy.

Left: *A sea monster photographed off Hook Island, Australia, December 1964*

Wild Children

MOTHERED BY ANIMALS

Every decade there are two or three strange cases of children lost in the wild who are apparently adopted by animals, who live with them and adopt their ways and who exist on a diet of raw meat and sometimes grass and herbs.

Amala and Kamala
The inhabitants of the Indian village of Midnapore begged a travelling missionary to rid them of an evil spirit that took the form of half man, half beast and emerged from the forest at night to stalk the village. The Reverend Joseph Singh set out with a party of villagers on 17 October 1920 to dig out the supposed lair of the 'man ghost'.

When the diggers began their work, two wolves broke cover and fled, but a third, a female, did her best to defend the lair until she was killed by the tribesmen. Two wolf cubs emerged next, followed by the creatures described by the Reverend Singh in his diary:

> Close after the cubs came the ghost – hand, foot and body like a human being; but the head was a huge ball of something covering the shoulders and the upper portion of the bust, leaving only a sharp contour of the face visible, and it was human. Close at its heels came another awful creature like the first, but smaller in size. Their eyes were bright and piercing, unlike human eyes.

The eyes may not have looked human in that first, frightened moment but the 'ghosts' turned out to be two little girls, probably abandoned in infancy by parents who could not face the expense of bringing up female children, raised by a wolf. They were unable to stand upright but could run fast on all fours and their sense of smell was highly developed, as though they had adapted to the natural life of the wolf, the wild hunter.

The Reverend Singh was able to stop the nervous villagers from harming the girls and he took them to an orphanage, where they were named Amala and Kamala. Though it was impossible to tell their age for certain, Kamala seemed 7 or 8 and Amala about 18 months younger. They were totally bewildered by their surroundings and by human company and for Amala the shock was too great; she died within a year. Kamala managed to adapt to some extent: at first she would only eat on all fours but gradually she learned to accept food from other children and then to use her own hands. She learned to stand upright and by the time she died, 9 years later, she had a vocabulary of about 30 words.

Right: When Amala and Kamala were found in the lair of a she-wolf they were unable to stand upright.
Far right: Some animals seem to sense the helplessness of the new born and treat human babies as their own.

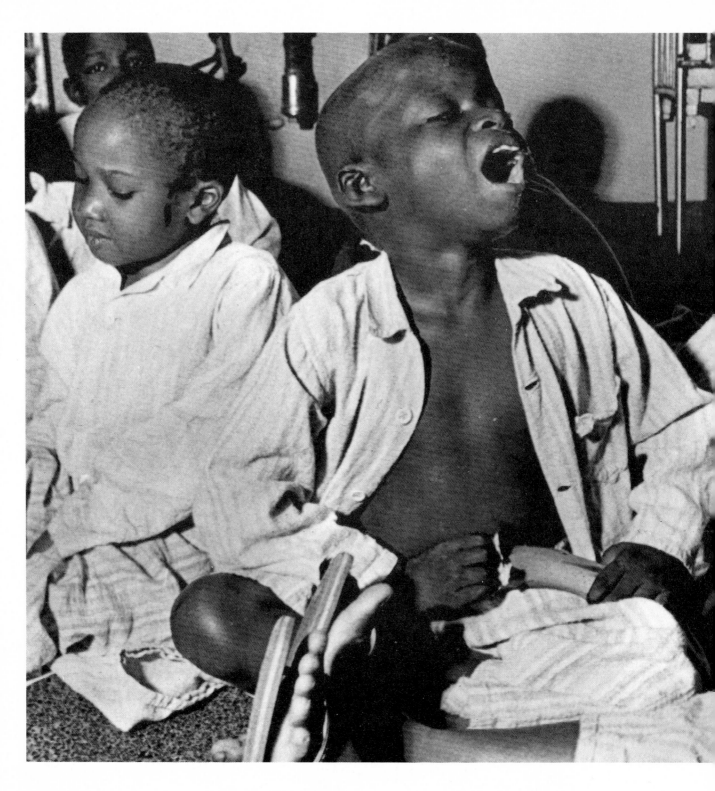

Above: The boy holding a banana was found in the jungle of Kenya by missionaries; they believe that he was raised by wild apes.

Other Wolf Children

Chambers' Journal, in the 19th century, reported the case of an Indian boy who had been lost, or abandoned, as a baby and was eventually found roaming happily with a pack of wolves. When he was returned to his family they found him completely unmanageable: he would growl and snarl, rejecting all human care and all through the night would wail like an animal. One night some of the villagers, angered by his constant noise, tied him to a tree. They said that two wolf cubs were attracted by his miserable cries and played around the tree-trunk all night, keeping him company and only making off back to the forest when dawn came. The boy lived for only a short time and never learned to speak or to respond to the people around him.

Another child at an orphanage was said to have been carried off by a she-wolf in 1843 while his mother worked nearby in the rice fields. Long after he had been

given up for dead, villagers 16 km (10 miles) away saw an unusual creature running with a litter of wolf cubs. It turned out to be the lost boy, identified by a burn scar on his knee.

In spite of all efforts, he could never eat cooked food or speak; his only form of communication was a low, animal growl. He was always unhappy and unwilling to adapt to normal human ways and he made several attempts to escape; eventually, in the spring of 1851, he made off into the jungles of Bhangapore and was never seen again.

Not all feral children find their homes with wolves. In 1973 a boy, apparently about 10 years old, was found living with a family of monkeys in the jungles of Sri Lanka. He could not stand upright or speak but he could run fast on all fours, climb trees nimbly and use either hands or feet to pick up objects, just like his monkey 'brothers and sisters'.

In 1967 a French anthropologist, Jean Claude Armen, discovered a boy running with a herd of wild gazelle in the Sahara desert, tracing him by his footprints in the sand. The child seemed to communicate perfectly with the gazelles, jumping about like them and even twitching his

ears at any unusual sound. Just like them he sniffed at the anthropologist and, when he was convinced that he posed no threat, he proceeded to lick him.

The boy, who seemed to be about 10 years old, lived on roots, unearthing them along with the herd, then peeling them with his teeth. Armen found that his teeth were worn level, like those of the herbivores. His ankles were thick and strong and he could match the incredible bursts of speed of the gazelles, as well as their bounding grace.

Children raised in the wild seem to adapt remarkably well to their harsh environment; they seem impervious to the extremes of heat and cold and learn to move just as fast as the animals around them. Wolf children like the girls of Midnapore develop a velvety skin texture and layers of hard, calloused skin on their elbows and knees as a result of walking on all fours. However, they usually find it impossible to make the transition back to civilized society. They hardly manage to adapt at all, learning only a couple of words, and they usually die before they reach their teens. Often the children seem to have been 'captured' rather than 'rescued'.

Right: This boy, whose hands and feet had to be tied to prevent escape, was found running with a herd of gazelles in the Syrian desert by Bedouins, who said that he ran faster than their jeep.

Living Fossils

TOADS ENTOMBED IN THE DARK

Workmen digging in Hartlepool, England, in 1865 cracked open a block of magnesium limestone, 8 m (25 ft) deep, to find a live toad in a hollow that exactly fitted its body.

The local paper reported that it was bright and lively and that it 'appeared desirous to perform the process of respiration but evidently experienced some difficulty and the only sign of success consisted of a 'barking' noise which it continues to make at present on being touched ... On minute examination its mouth was found to be completely closed, and the barking noise it makes proceeds from its nostrils.'

Other differences from normal local toads were the claws of the forefeet which turned inwards and the exceptionally long hind claws. When it was first released its colour was pale, like its limestone home – estimated to be several million years old – but it soon darkened to olive brown.

A Living Fossil

The toad was just one of a number of 'living fossils' discovered inside soil rock. Snakes, shellfish and frogs have all been found alive, and in 1818 a Cambridge geologist found three live newts along with a layer of fossilized newts and sea urchins in a chalk pit. Two died soon afterwards but the third was so lively that, once placed in water, it escaped.

Scientists have often tried to explain away this phenomenon, maintaining that the creatures probably crawled in through narrow cracks in the rock, became entombed when the rock shifted slightly and then went into a dormant state until they were discovered. However, some of the finds have been as far down as 183 m (200 yd), which seems a long way for a straying creature to crawl down a handy crack.

Various experiments have shown that toads can live entombed for long periods. One toad became famous throughout the USA after being sealed into the cornerstone of a municipal building in Eastland, Texas, in 1897 and emerging alive in 1928. Before that, in 1862, a French experiment encased 20 toads in plaster of Paris and buried them. Twelve years later, when the block was dug up again, four were still alive.

No one can say with certainty how old the 'living fossils' might be, but they often seem to exhibit different characteristics from known modern varieties, like the Hartlepool toad. A number have permanently sealed mouths, or no mouths at all, which suggests very lengthy entombment. This was the case with three Shropshire toads found in a cavity of solid crock when excavations for a new hospital were under way and with a toad sealed into the middle of a lump of coal found in Warwickshire.

Scientists debated the possible lifespan of the toad vigorously in Victorian times, often dismissing the reports as tall tales of the construction business, rather like the stories fishermen tell about the 'one that got away'. Since 1900 there have been few reports, possibly because modern methods of digging and construction make it less likely that anyone might discover and rescue the hapless creatures, but as recently as 1982 workmen in New Zealand hacked two frogs from lumps of rock 2 m (6½ ft) down. Both were moist to the touch and lively enough to hop away.

Right: The coelacanth is a 'living fossil' of the sea. Until 40 years ago scientists were convinced that these fish, once plentiful in the oceans of the world, had been extinct for 60 million years and the only records were the ancient fossils found in rocks. Then in 1938 a living coelacanth was netted in the Indian Ocean and rewards were offered for more specimens. This fish was found near the Comero islands where the locals were accustomed to drying and salting them.

Monsters of the Deep

SEAFARERS' HORROR STORIES

Stories of sea monsters have been told for as long as men have sailed the seas and though many can be dismissed as a result of too vivid an imagination or an over-generous rum ration, most experts admit that there could be unknown creatures of enormous proportions lurking in the depths of the ocean. Two-thirds of the earth's surface is covered by water and much of it has yet to be explored.

Classic Stories of Sea Monsters

One of the classic monster sightings was reported to the Lords of the Admiralty by the captain of the British frigate *Daedalus* in 1848. In the South Atlantic, the crew had watched 'a sea serpent of extraordinary dimensions' for about 20 minutes. At least 18 m (60 ft) was visible and the snake-like head rose 1.2 m (4 ft) out of the water. The captain stated in his report: 'Had it been a man of my acquaintance I should easily have recognized the features with the naked eye. It did not deviate from its course to the southwest which it held at the pace of 12 to 15 miles per hour, apparently on some determined purpose.'

Many other sober, reliable witnesses have risked ridicule by bringing home eye-witness reports of monsters. In 1905 Meade Waldo and Michael Nicoll, both respected members of the Royal Zoological Society, saw a mysterious creature from the deck of the steamship *Valhalla* off the coast of Brazil. Waldo wrote: 'I saw a large fin or frill sticking out of the water, dark seaweed brown in colour, somewhat crinkled at the edge. I could see under the water the shape of a considerable body. A great head and neck rose out of the water ahead of the frill. The neck was about the thickness of a man's body: the head had a turtle-like appearance, as had also the eye.'

Canada has its own monster, Cadborosaurus, or 'Caddy' for short, which has been sighted quite regularly off the coast of Vancouver. Captain Paul Sowerby saw it in 1939, its head standing 1.2 m (4 ft) above the water, with its fat, wrinkled body going down at least 12 m (40 ft). Fisherman David Webb, who saw it in 1941, described its head as being a bit like that of a camel. Judge James Brown saw it rise out of the water several times in 1950; he described it as a 14 m (45 ft) serpent.

A huge sea monster has been seen off Britain's Cornish coast many times since 1975 and has become known as 'Morgawr', or sea-giant. Two fairly clear photographs were taken in 1976 by a witness who described it as looking like an elephant waving its trunk, except that the 'trunk' was a long neck ending in a small, snake-like head. It was dark in colour, with skin like a sea-lion.

Top left: *A sea monster photographed in Stonehaven Bay off Hook Island, Australia, in December, 1964.* **Bottom left**: *In 1925 an enormous carcase excited great interest when it was washed ashore on the beach at Santa Cruz.* **Below**: *The sea serpent seen from the deck of the frigate Daedalus in 1848 became part of the official Admiralty records.*

Right: Archbishop Olaus Magnus mentioned this monster in his history of Scandinavia in 1555. **Far right**: An artist's impression of the dreaded Kraken attacking a sailing ship. **Below**: This picture of 'Morgawr', the Cornish sea monster, was taken near Falmouth in 1976.

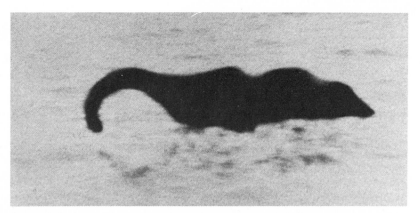

Far more dramatic was the appearance of the monster spotted by the crew of a German U-boat in the North Atlantic in 1915. They had torpedoed a British steamer, and immediately after it sank there was an underwater explosion. Out of the churning sea shot a huge, writhing creature about 18 m (60 ft) long. It was shaped like a crocodile, had four limbs with webbed feet and a long tail.

The monsters of the deep can be killers, according to some accounts. Five US Air Force divers were floating on a raft in thick fog off the Florida coast in 1962. Suddenly they began choking on a sickening smell and then they found 'an enormous head and neck' towering over them. Only one diver survived: as the raft capsized, his three friends were dragged down by the monster.

Giant Squid

The legendary Kraken, said to be large enough to seize ships and drag them down with its multiple arms, is now usually identified with a giant squid, which is large and fierce enough to attack and even sink ships. In the 1930s the 15,000 ton tanker *Brunswick*, travelling at 12 knots near Samoa, was attacked twice by a monster squid before the creature became entangled in the propeller and was cut to pieces. In the 19th century, *The Pearl*, a 150-ton schooner, was attacked while becalmed in the Bay of Bengal. The crew of another ship watched helplessly while giant tentacles seized the schooner and pulled it under the ocean.

Over the past century several squids measuring 6–9 m (20–30 ft) have been washed ashore on the beaches of Newfoundland, enabling scientists to study their fearsome tentacles, suckers and claws. One specimen, found in 1878, measured 18 m (60 ft) and a squid of a similar size was seen by oceanographers from the *San Pablo* off the coast of Newfoundland in 1966, with a sperm whale enmeshed in its tentacles. During the Second World War the crew of a ship in the Indian Ocean claimed to have had a clear view of a monster squid 53 m (175 ft) in length.

One of the most promising monster corpses was washed up on a beach in Florida, USA, in 1896. The mutilated body measured 6.4 m (21 ft) across and the skin was so thick that it was hard work penetrating it with an axe. One of the arms, lying nearby in the sand, measured over 10 m (32 ft). Observers calculated that if it was some kind of giant octopus, the whole creature would have been 61 m (200 ft) across.

Perhaps bathers on a tropical beach will one day find themselves staring down at the carcass of a sea serpent that will validate all the mariner's tales.

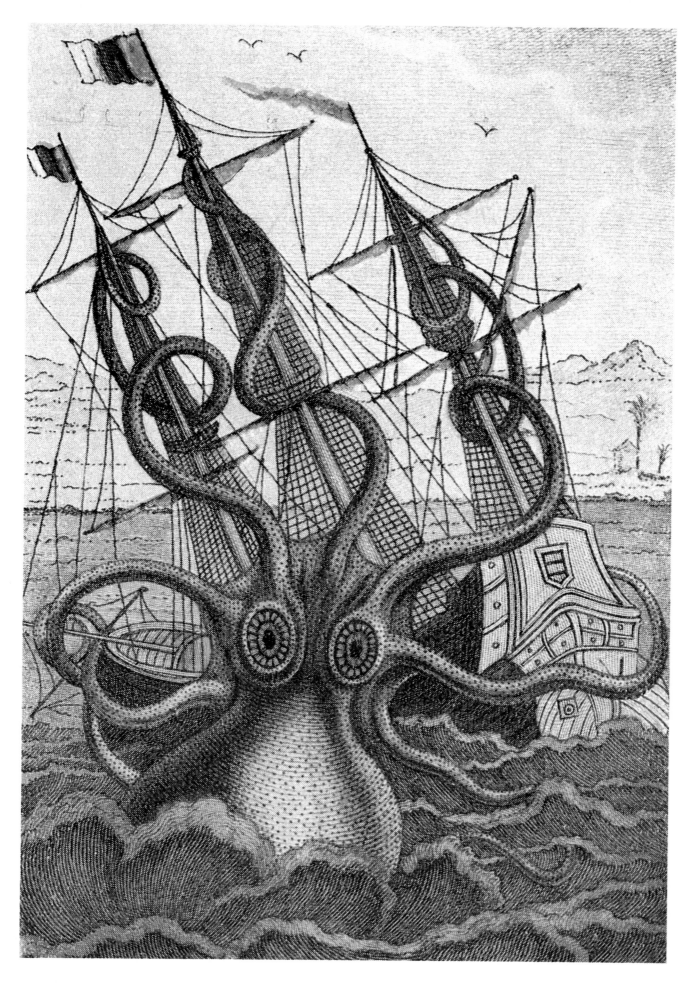

An enlargement of the 'monster' shows the serpent-like head described by Nessie spotters over the years.

The Loch Ness Monster

DOES NESSIE EXIST?

The first report of a monster in Loch Ness came in AD 565. St Columba and his followers were travelling along the loch on an evangelical mission. A strange beast suddenly rose from the water, only a few metres from him. St Columba, famed for his mastery over animals, faced the monster and commanded: 'Go thou no further, nor touch that man', and the monster dived deep into the loch.

Modern Sightings

It was only in 1933 that the spate of modern sightings began, after work started on building a new road along the shores of the loch which entailed blasting several tons of rock from the shore. Many supporters of the monster theory believe that the blasting destroyed the monster's ancient underwater lairs and left it roaming the open loch for the first time.

The furore began in March 1933 when John MacKay, a local hotel manager, was driving with his wife along the side of the mirror-smooth loch. Mrs MacKay saw a sudden eruption in the water as a great dark body surfaced about 100 m (328 ft) from the shore. At his wife's cry of amazement, Mr MacKay braked sharply and they both watched as the water churned and foamed and two large humps undulated above the water line.

Before the end of the year the first photo of Nessie appeared in national newspapers, along with statements by photographic experts confirming that there had been no evidence of tampering on the negative.

So, the Loch Ness monster, or 'Nessie', became internationally famous. Sightseers and scientists alike flocked to the loch in the hope of a glimpse. Inevitably, the hoaxers were there, too. In December 1933 an enormous footprint appeared, reckoned to belong to a powerful animal about 6 m (20 ft) long, but the story died when an Inverness museum, just a few kilometres from Loch Ness, reported that a mounted hippopotamus foot was missing from their natural history section.

Since the Second World War interesting accounts of sitings have included the following:

1951: Lachlan Stuart, a Forestry Commission employee living beside the loch took a photograph showing three humps sticking out of the water. The photo was found to be genuine.

1959: James Alexander, an AA patrolman, was making a call from a phone booth beside the loch when he turned to see the monster's head standing 2 m (7 ft) out of the water. He flagged down a passing lorry and the driver confirmed his account.

1961: More than a dozen guests at a hotel beside the loch watched for six minutes while a creature with two humps and a length of 9 m (30 ft) cavorted in the water.

1963: Two local fishermen suddenly found their boat rocking violently, though the surrounding water was calm. Then the head and neck of a unknown creature appeared about 25 m (82 ft) away, out of the water, with a mane of dark hair.

1973: Anthony Nicol Shiels, a professional psychic, photographed what he beleived to be Nessie surfacing 91 m (100 yd) from Castle Urquhart. His picture shows a thick neck and serpent-like head standing above the water.

Left: Jennifer Bruce noticed nothing unusual when she took a photograph of Urquhart Bay in Loch Ness but, when printed, the picture showed a strange creature in the centre.

Evidence for Nessie's Existence

One of the chief pieces of evidence for the monster's existence is the cine film taken by the aeronautical engineer turned Nessie-hunter, Tim Dinsdale, in April 1960 which seemed to show a hump-backed creature moving at about 16 km (10 miles) an hour. When the RAF's Joint Air Reconnaissance Intelligence Centre examined the film they found it genuine and, having ruled out the possibilities of boats and submarines, they decided that it was probably 'an animate object 3½–5 m (12–16 ft) long and 2 m (6½ ft) wide'.

Dinsdale's film led to the establishment of the Loch Ness Investigation Bureau, which began a systematic study of the loch. For 10 years investigators kept watch for long periods, but though they recorded many eye-witness reports and many sightings of their own, they never managed to take the definitive photograph of Nessie.

Sonar, which registers the sound waves transmitted by underwater objects, has been used by several teams of Loch Ness investigators since 1960 and has indicated that there are large moving objects deep in the loch.

Hydrophones let down into the loch have picked up strange sounds. In 1962 low frequency tapping sounds which seemed animal-like were recorded and in 1970 there were clicking sounds all over

Urquhart Bay, with no identifiable cause.

But after 40 years of intense interest focused on Loch Ness and a succession of investigative expeditions, there is still no undisputed evidence for the existence of a monster, though the sheer volume of eye-witness accounts is impressive. There are many explanations for these sightings however. Loch Ness is Britain's largest body of fresh water, 35 km (24 miles) long, with sheer mountains rising to 600 m (2000 ft) from the water's edge and light and shadow can play tricks with the eyes, distorting the size of objects seen in the distance. Boats are probably responsible for many mistaken sightings; the wake can show up as a wave on the calm water well after the boat has disappeared from sight.

The Plesiosaur

If there is a 'monster' in the loch, the favourite candidate is the plesiosaur, a giant reptile believed extinct for 70 million years. Museum reconstructions of plesiosaurs came remarkably close to eye-witness accounts of Nessie. The theory is that Nessie's ancestors were cut off from the sea when the loch was formed at the end of the last Ice Age and that the tremendous depth of the loch, up to 300 m (1000 ft), enabled the creatures to live and breed undisturbed in the murky depths.

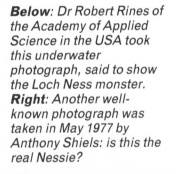

Below: *Dr Robert Rines of the Academy of Applied Science in the USA took this underwater photograph, said to show the Loch Ness monster.*
Right: *Another well-known photograph was taken in May 1977 by Anthony Shiels: is this the real Nessie?*

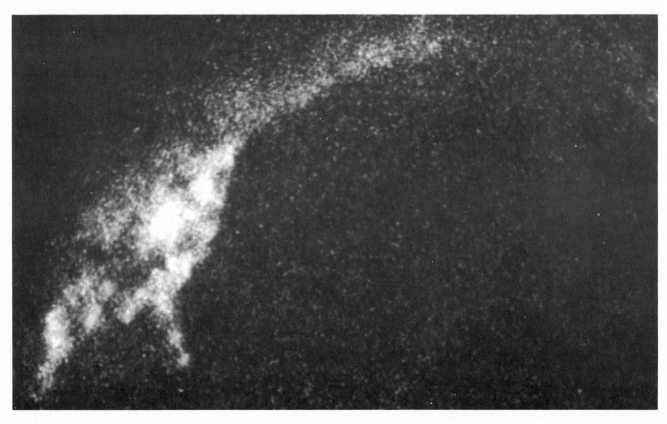

Merfolk

WILD CREATURES OF THE SEA

Merfolk, those strange and intriguing creatures, half human and half fish, are part of the folklore of many countries. The Irish believed they were pagans banished by St Patrick, while the Scandinavians thought they were fallen angels who lived in the sea as seals and, once on land, were allowed part human shape.

The Dangers of Seduction

A couple of centuries ago, every sailor was warned to beware of mermaids who were to be seen sitting on rocks, combing their long hair and singing seductively, trying to lure ships to their doom. Merfolk were the custodians of drowned souls, always eager to add to their company.

Columbus reported seeing three mermaids on his voyage in 1492 and Henry Hudson, sailing in the Arctic Ocean in 1607, described a creature that resembled a woman from the navel upwards but had a tail like that of a porpoise and speckled like a mackerel.

In 1917 the captain of the *Leonidas*, sailing from New York to Le Havre, reported in detail the sighting of a creature resembling a human being from the neck upwards, with black hair and white skin but with the form of a fish below the arms. It stayed alongside for about six hours, raising itself well out of the water for 15 minutes at a time to gaze at the watchers, then diving and appearing again on the other side of the ship. He wrote: 'No one on board ever saw the like fish before; all believe it to be a Mermaid.'

Merfolk seem to have been drawn to the peace of the Scottish coastline. In 1833 six Shetland fishermen found what they decided must be a mermaid caught in their nets off the island of Yell. When they drew her into the boat they found she was about a metre long, with the upper half of her body resembling a woman, though it was quite monkeyish in appearance. Her head had long bristles extending to the shoulders and she could raise and lower them, like a crest. The lower half of her body was like a fish but without scales. They kept her in the boat for three hours but she moaned so miserably all the time that eventually they took pity on her and put her back in the water.

The mermaid of Benbecula, in the Outer Hebrides, sounds a more attractive visitor. In 1830 locals cutting seaweed saw her frolicking in the sea and then, a few days later, her corpse was washed up on the beach. The upper half of her body was the size of a well-nourished child of three of four, though the breasts were too developed for those of a child. Her hair was long and dark, her skin soft and white to the waist, then the lower half of the body was shaped like a salmon, without scales. Many people saw the body, and Duncan Shaw, the well-respected factor and sheriff, certainly thought the creature human enough to order a shroud and coffin for her.

Modern Mermaids

A report of a mermaid came as recently as 1947 when an elderly fisherman claimed to have seen one off the Hebridean island of Muck. No scoffing or disbelief could ever change his mind about what he saw. Another modern sighting, this time of a merman, was reported in the state of Cochin, India, in 1937, when fishermen hauled a fair, handsome youth on to the beach. As a crowd gathered to watch, he writhed his way to the edge of the sea and swam away.

In 1881 a Boston newspaper reported that the body of a mermaid, well preserved, had been brought to New Orleans. Most such 'finds', however, were shown to be fakes, such as the one exhibited by a Boston captain in London in 1822. Doctors said of this that the head and trunk were those of apes, the breasts were artificially padded and that the lower half was that of a fish.

The modern explanation of the legend is that sailors too long at sea mistook marine mammals like the dugong or manatee for merfolk but it is difficult to imagine the groggiest sailor taking these chunky, ungainly creatures for humans, much less for seductive, long-haired women.

Merfolk, half human and half fish, have been part of the folk-lore of many countries over the centuries. **Left**: *A mermaid seducing a captive sailor.* **Above**: *A mermaid caught by three astounded fisherman.*

Yeti and Bigfoot
APE-MEN OF THE WILD

There are rumours of mysterious ape-men who inhabit the wild, unexplored mountain countries of China, Tibet, Russia and North America. The ape-man goes by many names: to the Americans he is Bigfoot, the Russians call him Alma and throughout the snowy Himalayas he is known as the Yeti, nicknamed the Abominable Snowman.

The Yeti

The Sherpas, the mountain people of the Himalayas, have always believed in the Yeti who live beyond the snowline, their bodies covered in thick, coarse hair, their features half human, half ape, standing up to 3.6 m (12 ft) high and walking upright. Sightings by Europeans in the first half of the 20th century were dismissed as figments of the imagination until the publication of photographs taken by mountaineer Eric Shipton in 1951. Shipton was climbing with the British surgeon Michael Ward and Sherpa Sen Tensing in an unexplored area 48–64 km (30–40 miles) west of Mount Everest when they came across a series of clear footprints on a glacier. Attempts to explain these away as the tracks of known animals, distorted by melting snow, have never succeeded and the pictures remain one of the best pieces of hard evidence for the existence of the Yeti.

Bigfoot or 'Sasquatch'

The Bigfoot of North America, often known by his Indian name of *Sasquatch*, is more obliging than the Yeti about personal appearances. Early settlers were told by local tribes about the creatures covered in reddish-brown hair, standing anything from 2–3 m (6–10 ft) tall, walking on two legs, with a receding forehead and almost no neck.

Above: A Yeti scalp is one of the items of proof produced by the Sherpas. *Right*: Eric Shipton, leader of the British expedition of 1951, took this photograph of a clear line of Yeti footprints. *Left*: A pick set alongside a footprint shows its enormous size.

Below: A frame from the famous film taken at Bluff Creek. **Right**: Casts made from the Bluff Creek footprints.

encased in ice. It appeared to have been shot through the back of the head and one story was that it was shot trying to attack a girl in the Minnesota woods. Another was that the block of ice containing the body had been found floating in the sea.

Heuvelmans, who said that he could even smell the decomposition where melting ice had exposed a little of the flesh, was convinced that this was 'a previously unknown form of living hominid' and called it *Homo Poingodes*. The scientific establishment disagreed, certain that it was a rubber dummy. When they wanted to carry out proper tests they found that the owner had taken the ice man on tour again.

Thousands of Americans had the chance to view the ice man in fairgrounds but all that now remains are the reports and photographs made by Heuvelmans and his colleagues, who were convinced that the corpse was genuine, probably shot in Vietnam and smuggled back to America along with the bodies of war victims.

Giants in the USSR

In the Soviet Union, many reports of unknown, man-like creatures have come from the Caucasus and Pamir mountains, though the Russian Alma is rather different from the Yeti, less like a beast and more like a man. In 1964 Dr Jeanne Koffman set up a permanent study centre in the Caucasus to sift the local evidence and built up a mass of eye-witness evidence as well as casts of footprints, samples of hair and dung.

In 1925 Major-General Mikhail Topilsky and his troops were following a band of White Army soldiers fleeing across the Pamir mountains near the Afghan border. They followed a trail of footsteps leading to a cave and, when no one responded to their warnings, they fired into the opening.

The creature that staggered out, mortally wounded, was the size and shape of a man, yet the whole body was covered in hair, the jaws were large and protruding, the forehead receding. The army doctor who examined the body pronounced it 'not human' and the soldiers left the body where it had fallen.

In the past, the Soviet authorities have been wary of letting out too much information about Alma reports, fearing ridicule from the west. In January 1988, however, the Soviet Ministry of Culture announced an official expedition to track down the Alma, 'man's nearest cousin'. Perhaps, at long last, some conclusive proof of his existence will come to light.

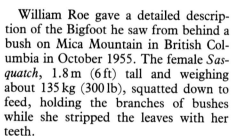

William Roe gave a detailed description of the Bigfoot he saw from behind a bush on Mica Mountain in British Columbia in October 1955. The female *Sasquatch*, 1.8 m (6 ft) tall and weighing about 135 kg (300 lb), squatted down to feed, holding the branches of bushes while she stripped the leaves with her teeth.

Then came the 1967 film taken by Roger Patterson, a rancher who went hunting for Bigfoot with a part-Indian friend, at Bluff Creek in northern California. As they emerged into a clearing by the creek they saw a female Bigfoot less than 91 m (400 ft) away and, before it loped off into the forest, Patterson was able to shoot 9 m (30 ft) of colour film as well as taking plaster casts of footprints. The film was shown worldwide and has been examined exhaustively by experts, without ever being proved to be a fake.

The Ice Man

Some instances of sightings, however, come in for their share of ridicule. In 1968 zoologist Dr Bernard Heuvelmans heard of a fairground exhibit, known as the Ice Man, owned by an ex-Air Force pilot. The body of an unknown creature 1.8 m (5ft 10 in) tall, broad and muscular, with short legs and broad flat feet, lay

Vampires

THE PROWLING UNDEAD

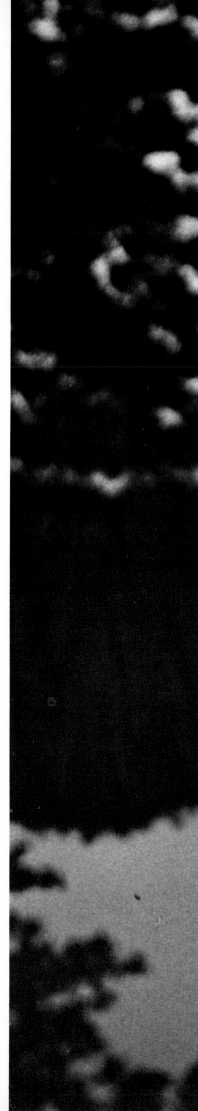

In films, the most famous vampire of them all, Count Dracula, stalks the surroundings of his sinister Transylvanian castle by night, ready to sink his pointed teeth into the neck of his unfortunate victims and drink their blood.

Blood Suckers

The fictional Dracula was based on accounts of vampires – the undead who rise from their graves at night to suck the blood of the living as they lie asleep – which spread terror through Central and Eastern Europe, particularly in the 18th century.

It was widely believed that sorcerers, suicides, murderers and those who had been bitten by vampires all turned into vampires after death. In some areas this was supposed to extend to anyone who died in the 'unclean' days between Christmas and Epiphany, when evil ruled the earth. Great care was taken to guard an unburied corpse, for vampires could also be created if a cat jumped over the body or even if the shadow of a living man fell across it.

The word 'vampire' was only introduced into the English language at the beginning of the 18th century as constant reports of the creatures' grisly work arrived from Hungary, Moravia, Poland and Silesia.

Many learned theological treatises were written on the subject and John Heinrich Zopfius, in 1733 gave a classic description:

Vampires issue forth from their graves in the night, attack people sleeping quietly in their beds, suck out all their blood from their bodies and destroy them. They beset men, women and children alike, sparing neither age nor sex. Those who are under the fatal malignity of their influence complain of suffocation and a total deficiency of spirits, after which they soon expire.

Creatures without Shadows

Vampires were supposed to cast no shadow and were not reflected in mirrors: so long as they kept out of sunlight and away from looking glasses, however, there was no sure way to tell a vampire from a man, though they were supposed to have deathly pale skin and full red lips. Their bodies were gaunt and emaciated, except when they had just drunk their fill of blood, when they became plump and bloated. In Bulgaria, they were said to have only one nostril; in Poland their tongues ended in a sharp point.

Above: *Vampires could only be killed by a stake driven through the heart.*

Right: *The silent film* Nosferatu, *made in 1921, was an early vampire movie.*

Right: Vampires have been portrayed on stage and screen as semi-comic figures. **Below**: The name Dracula came from a 15th century ruler of Wallachia, known for his barbarous acts.

A Stake Through the Heart

Vampires could only be detected for certain once the grave was opened up, because the body would be uncorrupted, the eyes open, the cheeks pink and the chest full of fresh blood. The accepted method of disposing of the dread creature was driving a stake of aspen (the wood supposedly used for Christ's cross) or whitethorn (said to have made up the crown of thorns) through the body.

It was fear of vampires that led to the custom of suicides being buried at crossroads with a stake through their hearts. This practice was so prevalent that it was made illegal in England in 1824.

In 1727 a high-powered delegation was sent from Belgrade to the Yugoslavian village of Meduegna to investigate a vampire reign of terror. Several people reported that Arnold Paole, a young man who had died in a farming accident some weeks before, was roaming the village at night. Those who saw him soon took to their beds, pale and lethargic, and some had already died.

In his *History of Magic* in 1854, Ennemoser describes the scene when Paole's grave was opened 10 weeks after his burial:

It was seen that the corpse had moved to one side, the jaws gaped wide open and the blue lips were moist with new blood which had trickled in a thin stream from a corner of the mouth. All unafraid, the old sexton caught the body and twisted it straight. 'So,' he cried, 'you have not wiped your mouth since last night's work' ... the vampire ... looked indeed as though he had not been dead a day. On handling the corpse the scarfskin came off, and below that were new skin and new nails.

Garlic was scattered over the body and a whitethorn stake driven through his heart, at which Paole let out a fearsome shriek. Four of his victims were also disinterred and rendered harmless.

A few years later there was another outbreak of vampirism in the same area and this time all the graves in the cemetery were opened. A report by reputable officials and surgeons, dated 1732, recorded a whole list of apparent vampires, including a woman who had been buried for 100 days and was looking fitter and plumper than in real life, a 20-year-old woman buried for three months, whose body showed no sign of decay and whose loose skin came off her hands and feet to show fresh new skin and nails, and a 10-year-old girl whose body, when pierced with a stake, poured out warm blood.

Human Bloodsuckers

Today, although we might think we are free from such superstitions, we still have our vampires. They are psychotic killers who crave the taste of blood. Lorry-driver Peter Kürten, the 'monster of Dusseldorf' was sentenced to death in April 1931 after terrorizing the area for years, strangling his victims and cutting their throats. 'I need blood as others need alcohol,' he said. John George Haigh, tried at Sussex Assizes in 1949, killed nine people, always slitting their throats and drinking a glass of their blood. Both were convinced that they had done nothing wrong.

Below: Hungarian actor Bella Lugosi made a convincing and sinister Count Dracula in the 1931 film.

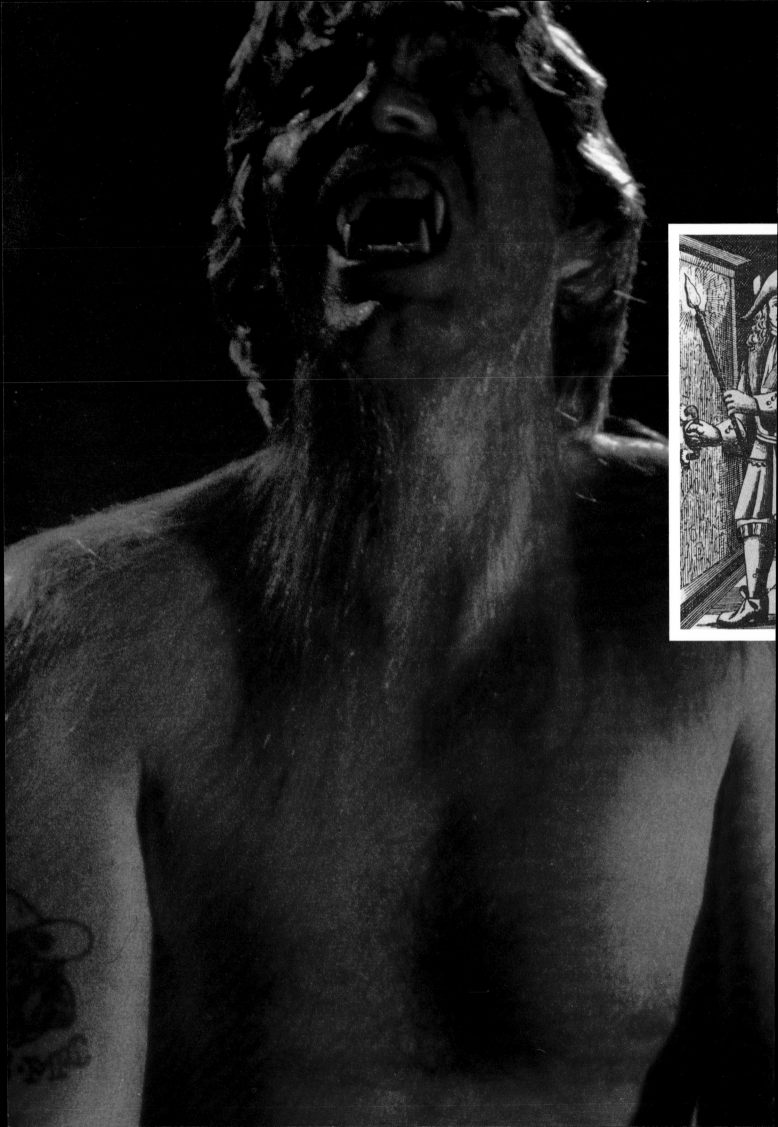

Werewolves

CHANGING FROM MAN TO WOLF

Above: *This engraving by Jacob Schneider shows a werewolf plaguing Eschenbach in Germany in 1685.* **Left**: *In the film* The Howling, *humans turned into werewolves when they were sexually excited.*

In the 16th century the fear of werewolves was so great that anyone who came under suspicion was literally ripped apart, because of the belief that to conceal themselves in the daytime they wore their wolf hair on the inside of their normal skin. Between 1520 and 1630, 30,000 cases were reported in Europe.

The belief in werewolves, that is, men who change into the shape of wolves and, like their wild counterparts, kill and eat human beings, has been deep-rooted for centuries. The werewolf of legend may change into animal form either accidentally or on purpose, but once changed he is distinguishable from a real wolf only by his human voice and eyes.

Werewolves could sometimes be caught by someone hiding their clothes, which prevented them from resuming their human shape. But they could only be killed or wounded by the use of a silver bullet or silver blade. Once hurt or killed they immediately returned to human form and any wound sustained as a wolf would be reproduced on their human bodies – the loss of an ear, an eye or a bullet wound in the side.

Werewolves were doubly dangerous because after death they turned into vampires and began a whole new reign of terror.

There are two alternative dictionary definitions of 'lycanthropy': it is either 'the power of changing oneself into a wolf' or 'a form of madness, in which the patient imagines himself to be a wolf'. Scientists today prefer to believe that any recorded histories of werewolves were examples of madness: murderers who killed believing themselves to be wolves, reinforcing the credulous public's belief in their magical transformation.

Jacques Rollet

In 1598 Jacques Rollet, the man-wolf of Caude, in France, was tried and condemned for murder. Villagers gave evidence that they had discovered three wolves mauling the dead body of a teenage boy. The wolves ran off into the forest but the men gave chase and soon found the long-haired and bearded Rollet, his hands covered with blood, shreds of human flesh hanging from his claw-like nails. He confessed that he was able to change himself into a wolf by means of a salve and that with two friends, also werewolves, he had attacked the boy. The other wolves, whether animal or human, were never brought to justice.

At the turn of the 16th century, an area of Bordeaux was being terrorized by what was thought to be a wild beast and several young girls were killed. When little Margaret Poiret was attacked by a creature she said looked like a wolf, though it was shorter and broader, with a smaller head than usual, she bravely beat it off with a stick.

When a retarded teenage boy called Jean Grenier was brought to trial, everyone in the region breathed a sigh of relief. He had bragged to other youngsters that he could turn himself into a wolf, with the aid of a special salve, and he soon confessed to eating several girls. No one who heard him doubted that he firmly believed himself a werewolf but the President of the Court, who was not of a credulous disposition, decided that Grenier was suffering from hallucinations and should be locked up in an asylum.

In the 20th century, we may think we are too sophisticated to believe in the existence of real werewolves. Nevertheless, the legend, if legend it is, dies hard and reports of the dreaded 'man-wolf' still surface from time to time in the more remote areas of Europe.

Siamese Twins

THE CLOSEST UNION

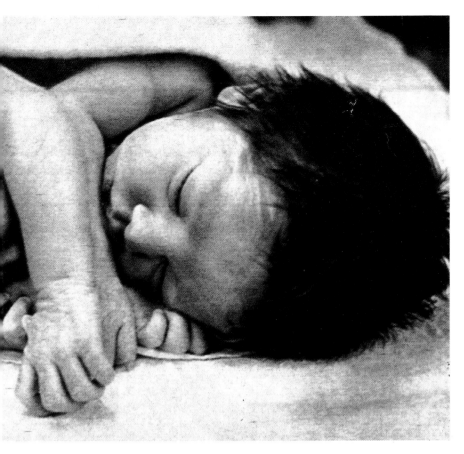

Far left: Eng and Chang were joined by a band of flesh at the breastbone. **Above**: Today, doctors can usually separate Siamese twins.

The 'original' Siamese twins, the pair who gave their name to the phenomenon, were Eng and Chang, who were born in Siam in May 1811 and were joined at the chest.

They narrowly escaped death as infants, for the King of Siam saw them as omens of bad luck for the kingdom and was about to have them killed. However, a Scottish merchant saw their potential as a money-making exhibit and took them to America, where they were a sensation. A tour of Europe, which included a visit to London in November 1829, made them world famous, and wherever they went surgeons were keen to examine them and debate the possibilities of separation, though the operation was never attempted.

Later Eng and Chang retired to North Carolina to a quieter life of farming and, at the age of 44, they married English sisters Sarah Ann and Adelaide Yates. To satisfy the conventions of the day they installed their wives in different houses, visiting each for a week at a time; the arrangement seemed to work well, for between them they fathered 21 children.

Eng and Chang were by no means carbon copies of one another. From the beginning Eng was weak and sickly, while Chang was robust and lively. Later in life Chang often drank too much, though Eng disapproved strongly of

drunkenness. Chang tended to be quarrelsome and violent when drunk and once only escaped a jail sentence for assault because the judge was reluctant to jail the inoffensive Chang along with his brother.

In spite of their differences, Eng and Chang were very tolerant and loving towards one another; people who knew them marvelled at the way they managed to make the best of a difficult life, making it 'far more agreeable than a casual observer would suppose possible'. On 17 January 1874 they both died, apparently of old age.

Help for Siamese Twins

Modern technology means that Siamese twins born today can usually be separated soon after birth, but a century ago such operations were rare. In 1881 Swiss surgeons managed to separate four-month-old sisters, though one baby died six hours after the operation and the other a day later.

Later came the amazing attempt by a Parisian surgeon to separate the young Orissa sisters, born in India in 1889 and taken to Europe to be exhibited in peep shows and circuses at the age of four – amazing because the separation took place in the Paris circus as the climax to a gala evening. Cameras were there to photograph every stage of the operation. Sadly, though, the children died.

Siamese twins who spent their whole lives joined together often managed to carry on their individual lives with remarkable success. Rosa and Josefa Blazek, born in Czechoslovakia in 1880, were joined at the lower and back pelvis and had two hearts, two pairs of lungs but only one stomach. They became a threesome when Rosa married a German officer and in 1908 she had a baby boy. Her husband was killed in the First World War and the twins went on to earn a small fortune in travelling peep shows.

Each woman had her own distinct personality and widely differing tastes: Josefa always drank beer while Rosa drank wine, which resulted in frequent stomach upsets. Though they quarrelled often, the bond between them, psychological as well as physical, was so strong that when Josefa fell ill in 1922, Rosa refused to allow surgeons to attempt to separate them. 'If Josefa dies I want to die too,' she told them.

She did everything she could to save her sister, eating extra in an attempt to restore her strength, but when Josefa died Rosa followed suit within 15 minutes of her twin.

Freaks of Nature

TRAPPED IN EXTRAORDINARY BODIES .

Above: *General Tom Thumb and his wife were only 1 metre (40 in) tall.*
Top right: *Pascal Pinon, born in France in 1887, had a second head growing from his brow.*
Bottom right: *This two-headed gopher snake is a freak of the animal world.*

Sometimes nature seems to play cruel tricks which result in strange mutations, extra limbs or even heads for a few unfortunate individuals. The men and women trapped inside these freak bodies produce reactions of amazement or revulsion from others and have often found it impossible to live normal lives. They have settled for displaying their deformities in side-shows or circuses.

Lazarus-Johannes Baptista Colleredo toured throughout Europe in the 17th century, displaying the parasite half-body that seemed to grow out of his stomach. The second body, probably that of a twin who failed to develop

normally, sometimes seemed to move and saliva dribbled from the corner of its mouth, but its eyes remained permanently closed. Two centuries later Laloo, born in India, drew the crowds in America because he had a second trunk, with two extra arms and legs growing out of his chest.

Some sights were judged too horrific to be seen by the public and in the 1830s the French authorities banned a couple from Sardinia from exhibiting their baby twins, born with two upper bodies on a single trunk. A similar case of two girls with a single trunk, from which their bodies grew at right angles, was recorded in Montreal, Canada in 1878. They functioned independently to some extent, for one baby might be crying from hunger while the other slept peacefully.

The Tocci Brothers

The Italian Tocci brothers, born in 1877, were two distinct people from the chest up but had only one pair of legs between them. Christened Giovanni and Giacomo, each twin had well-formed head and arms and his own personality and reactions but were unable to walk because each could control only one leg.

Other Freaks

The skull of a four-year-old boy, at the Royal College of Surgeons in London, shows that the child, born in Bengal, India, in the 19th century, had two heads. One head grew on top of the other, each with nose, mouth, eyes and ears. There was even a report from doctors in Catania in 1834 of a child born with two necks, one with a single head and the other with two heads, all of them fully developed.

Far more common, and far less difficult to adapt to a tolerable lifestyle, are extra legs. Doctors believe that these extra limbs may result from an egg which fails to divide properly within the mother to produce identical twins.

Louise L., whose full name was never revealed, was born in 1869 with two extra, atrophied legs hanging between her own normal ones. She became rich by exhibiting herself all over France as the four-legged woman, as well as marrying and producing two normal babies.

Francesco Lentini, born in Sicily in 1889, had a third leg jutting from the right side of his body and doctors were reluctant to attempt to remove it in case the operation resulted in paralysis. When his family moved to America they resisted all offers from promoters and insisted that he should have a good educa-

tion, but he later chose to join a circus.

He was a cheerful man with a keen sense of humour who used to say that he always bought two pairs of shoes and gave the extra left one to a one-legged friend. He used his third leg, which was 5 cm (2 in) shorter than the others, as a stool and joked that he was the only man who had a built-in chair. The extra limb was no handicap; he could run and jump, roller-skate, cycle, ride a horse and drive a car.

He married, fathered four normal children and continued to tour the country with top companies such as Barnum and Bailey, Buffalo Bill's Wild West Show and the Walter Main Circus. When he died in Tennessee at the age of 77, he was the longest-living three-legged man ever.

CHAPTER FIVE

MYSTERIES
OF THE
UNIVERSE

◆

There is so much
that is unexplained in our universe:
gigantic monuments to past civilizations
hint at a vast body of lost knowledge, an
invisible energy force seems to give sacred
sites some magnetic power, lines drawn in
the deserts of Peru leave no clues
to their purpose.
Modern scientific advances fail to
provide answers when unidentified objects
hover overhead or frogs rain from the sky.
All we can do is to sift the evidence and
evaluate eye-witness accounts,
remembering how thin the line between
fact and fantasy can be.

Left: Horsehead nebula NGC 2024 in Orion.

Black Holes

ANTI-MATTER IN SPACE

Black holes are one of the great enigmas of space and we have hardly begun to tackle the questions they pose. They are like giant whirlpools in space, ready to suck in anything that comes near their force. American physicist John Wheeler calls them 'the greatest crisis ever faced by physics'. They seem to go against all the laws of science.

Holes in Space

Black holes are formed by the death of a massive star which has exhausted its fuel and collapsed inwards. The weight of the collapse compresses the dying star so that it shrinks smaller and smaller, becoming ever more dense. The gravitational pull of this small, dense object is so great that nothing can escape from it, even rays of light, so that once a star turns into a black hole it becomes invisible.

The black hole phenomenon was discovered as scientists investigated 'dead' stars. These included 'white dwarfs', that is, stars with less than four times the mass of the sun which shrink into a ball with the radius of the earth, so dense that a teaspoonful would weigh several tons. Stars with about four solar masses die in a more spectacular way: the star erupts in a great explosion known as a 'supernova'. Sometimes they blow themselves to bits, sometimes they leave behind a stellar core known as a neutron star. However, if the remnant core is two-and-a-half times as massive as the sun, it cannot remain as a neutron star. Its own gravity is too strong, it collapses in on itself and a black hole is born.

This, at least, is the theory but so much is conjecture that most scientists admit that the entire concept of black holes might be disproved in the future.

If a black hole is a member of a binary star system, it may continue orbiting a companion star that is still shining normally. Gas emitted by the companion star is sucked in by the gravitational pull of the black hole, becoming intensely heated and giving off X-rays, which can be detected by observation satellites.

Anything swallowed up by a black hole has no chance of escape; it would be sucked inexorably towards the centre. In theory, a man's body inside a black hole would be stretched to infinite length, as the gravitational pull on his feet (supposing he were falling feet first) would be so much greater than the pull on his head and shoulders. In fact, the tremendous force of gravity would tear him to pieces and his remains would be crushed smaller and smaller until they ceased to exist.

In our time, the interval between falling past the horizon of a black hole a million times as heavy as the sun would be a mere 10 seconds. Even in a black hole a billion times as heavy as the sun it would only take a few hours. However, as the normal rules of time are apparently suspended inside a black hole, who knows how long it might really take?

Students of space like to wonder what would happen if an astronaut could survive entry into a black hole and emerge unscathed on the other side. As black holes defy all conventional physical laws, would he find himself in a different universe, or would he travel backwards in time?

Solving the Energy Crisis

Some scientists talk of a time when we might use black holes to solve the world's energy crisis, perhaps even creating black holes artificially. Ideas of 'harvesting' black holes are still in the realms of science fiction – but then so was space travel in the not-so-distant past. There may come a day when the human race is so desperate for new forms of energy that it might seem worth braving the dangers of the black hole to find one.

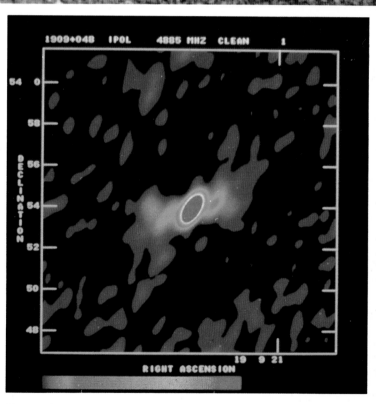

Stars of the M87 galaxy influenced by the gravitational field of a black hole. **Inset**: A radio map of SS 433, a double star system.

Unidentified Flying Objects

CLOSE ENCOUNTERS OF THE THIRD KIND

Sightings of UFOs are nothing new; in the 13th century the monks of St Albans saw a 'kind of large ship, elegantly shaped and of marvellous colour' in the sky above them and the monks of Byland Abbey, Yorkshire, recorded seeing a 'large, round, silver disc' in the sky. There have been other scattered reports through the centuries but since the Second World War there has been a flood of sightings. It has been calculated that if all the reports of UFOs were genuine there would have been as many as 3 million landings in the past 25 years!

Flying Saucers

On a bright June day in 1947 an experienced American pilot, Kenneth Arnold, was flying near Mount Rainier in Washington State, searching for the wreck of an aircraft that had crashed in the area, when he saw a chain of strange-looking aircraft, flying erratically. They were like no military or civilian aircraft Arnold had ever seen as they flew in a diagonal chain formation. There were nine altogether and he calculated that their wingspan was at least 30 m (100 feet) across and their speed at least 1,930 km/h (1,200 mph) at a time when aircraft seldom clocked 965 km/h (600 mph).

When he told the story later, Arnold described the craft as flying 'like you'd take a saucer and skip it across the water'. The 'Flying Saucers' of the newspaper headlines caught the public imagination and became part of the English language.

Dr Hynek has divided close encounters with UFOs into three categories: the first is simply a close sighting, the second is where the UFO leaves 'measurable physical effects on the land and on animate and inanimate objects', such as in the New Mexico incident, and the third when there is some contact between humans and UFO occupants.

These 'close encounters of the third kind' receive plenty of publicity and are vigorously disputed, such as the case of Betty and Barney Hill, who were driving through New Hampshire on a clear, starlit night when they saw a bright light and stopped the car to investigate. Two hours later they awoke with no memory of what had happened but later, under hypnosis, they told an amazing story of being taken aboard a spaceship and put through a thorough medical examination. They even drew maps of the charts they had seen on the walls of the spacecraft, maps that included stars unknown to astronomers.

Left: *UFO photographed at Conisborough, South Yorkshire.*

Above: *UFO photographed over Mexico City.*

The Broadhaven Triangle

Certain areas of Britain have reported a plethora of UFO sightings. In the 'Broadhaven triangle', an area in mid-Wales, 50 were recorded in a single year. The Coombs family found their car pursued by a small glowing ball that skimmed along the tops of the hedges and later they were terrified by a towering figure in a silver suit, with a luminous glow, standing at their front room window. When it disappeared it left them with a burned out TV set and a scorched rose bush. Louise Bassett, wife of a Carmarthen restaurant owner, saw flashing lights in the sky as she was driving home one night and her car radio cut out, at the same time as did dozens of other radios and televisions in the area. Fifteen Broadhaven primary school children left their football match and ran to tell their headmaster that they had seen a spaceship in the sky. Suspecting a hoax, he split them up and asked them to draw what they had seen and was astonished by the similarity of their drawings. Years later, none of the children had changed their story.

Other Sightings of UFOs

In the 1960s, UFO watchers flocked to Warminster in Wiltshire, where there were dozens of reports of cars stalling, electrical equipment cutting out and animals panicking as a glowing, cigar-shaped 'thing' was seen in the sky. Terry Pell almost crashed his lorry in the early hours of the morning as a crimson ball flew straight at his windscreen and Neil Pike, a bank security officer, was one of a group of UFO watchers who spotted what looked like low-flying spacecraft and two tall, shadowy figures. As Pike walked towards them they disappeared from his view, though the rest of the party watched him walk straight through them.

The more colourful accounts of close encounters leave disbelievers scoffing and one American researcher has offered a long-standing reward for anyone who returns from a meeting with an alien with the smallest souvenir, the equivalent of a paper clip oor box of matches, which could not have been made on earth. So far he has never had to pay out.

A group called Ground Saucer Watch in Phoenix have listed over 100 objects able to move across the sky at night, from fireflies to space satellites, from weather balloons to rockets. The planet Venus has been mistaken for a spacecraft so often that it has earned the nickname 'Queen of the UFOs'. British physicist R. V. Jones says that after plotting the movements of Venus it is often possible to predict the nights when reports of UFOs will stream in.

Obviously, many sightings can be explained away as wishful thinking, an over-active imagination or an honest mistake; but others, however, cannot be dismissed so easily.

In 1954 the captain of the BOAC aircraft *Centaurius*, approaching Labrador on a journey from New York to London, saw a dark object emerging from the clouds, surrounded by six smaller objects, apparently flying in parallel. He reported to the authorities on the ground and two fighters were sent up but just as one of the fighter pilots radioed that he saw the unknown objects on his radar screen, the smaller objects formed into single file and seemed to enter the larger object, which then disappeared. The phenomenon was witnessed by the 8 crew and 14 of the 51 passengers.

The Most Famous UFO

One of the most famous UFO incidents came in 1978 when an Australian film crew led by television reporter Quentin Fogarty took a night flight from South Island, New Zealand, to Wellington to check out the story of a UFO that had followed another plane a few nights before. When they saw bright lights in the sky over the north-east coast, ground control in Wellington confirmed that unidentified objects had registered on the radar screen. On the return journey, something described as having a transparent dome and a brilliantly lit base appeared on the starboard side of the plane, then suddenly shot in front of it and disappeared below it. Again, the object was seen on the ground radar.

Far left: UFO causes water vapour to condense into cloud formation. Left: A spinning UFO near Merlin, Oregon. Below: This US Air Force plane was followed by a UFO, which is shown in close-up on the insert.

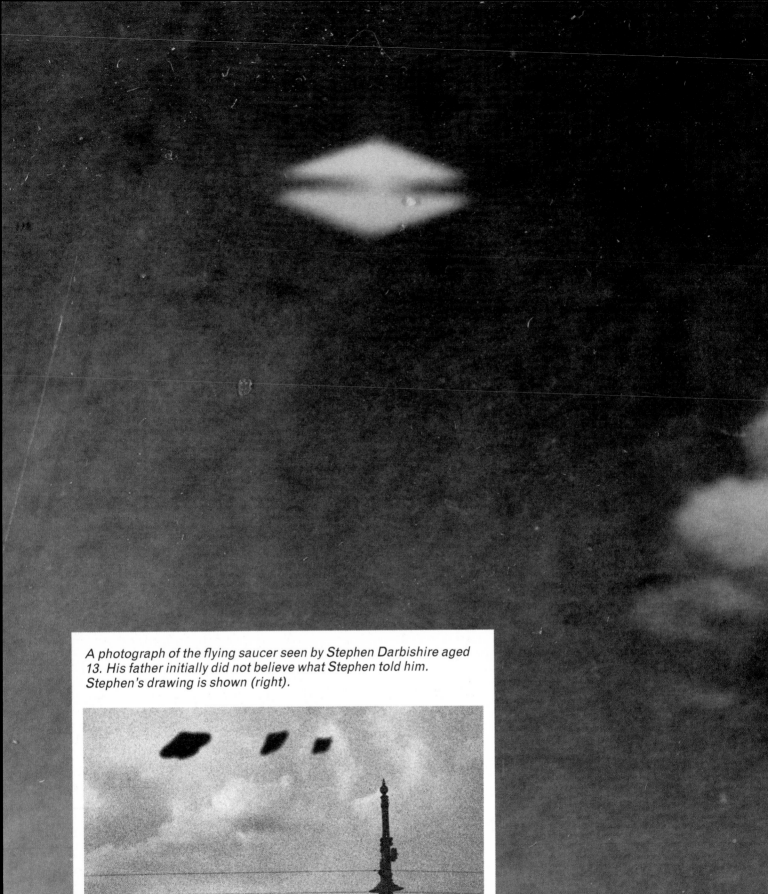

A photograph of the flying saucer seen by Stephen Darbishire aged 13. His father initially did not believe what Stephen told him. Stephen's drawing is shown (right).

When the film taken that night was shown, all sorts of theories were put forward to explain it away, the favourites being the planet Venus and the reflected lights of a Japanese fishing fleet in the area. A detailed investigation was carried out by the US Navy physicist Dr Bruce Maccabee but he found that Venus was not visible at the time and the fleet was too far away for its lights to play tricks on the sky. In the end, no convincing explanation was forthcoming.

The Australian film led to an epidemic of sightings all over the world. All round Britain strange lights were seen in the sky, in northern Italy dozens of villages were plunged into darkness as a UFO hovered overhead, several Israelis experienced close encounters with a red glowing object and a South African claimed a meeting with six spacemen on the road to Johannesburg.

Since the US government's investigation into UFOs, *Project Blue Book*, earned itself a bad name by trying to explain away every incident (even when explanations bordered on the absurd) and was disbanded in 1969, serious research has been left to private organizations. Officially, governments take a sceptical line, though it is known that the US armed forces have drawn up procedures to deal with UFOs.

Organizations such as Project Starlight International in Texas, with its wealth of sophisticated equipment, claims some important sightings, including a possible UFO that hovered over the laboratory for ten minutes on 10 December 1975. They took 4 photographs of the object, which has never been satisfactorily explained.

Where Do They Come From?

If UFOs do exist, where do they come from? They are usually supposed to be visitors from another planet but scientists point out that the nearest star system to ours that *could* support life is Alfa Centauri, and that even if the inhabitants could construct spacecraft capable of speeds beyond our wildest dreams, a round trip to Earth would still take something around 100 years.

Wherever they come from, their motives in coming here are still a puzzle: why should they call in on us, decade after decade, without making any effective contact? There are many theories: they are simply observing our habits, rather like us watching animals in the zoo; they are checking out the planet for eventual colonization; or they are collecting occasional specimens to take home.

American physicist Dr Stanton Friedman believes that UFOs are only safeguarding their own interests. 'They are not interested in settling here, they are just worried about what we will do when we get out there. They know it is only a matter of time – say about 100 years – before we send out starships and attempt to become part of the Galactic Federation. Before that happens, they want to know everything about us.'

Stonehenge
AN INVISIBLE POWERHOUSE OF ENERGY

Medieval tradition held that Stonehenge, the great brooding circle of stone rising from the bleak expanse of Salisbury Plain, was created by the mystic powers of the magician Merlin. It was said that the stones originally stood on a mountain in Ireland, brought there by a vanished race of giants and that they were transported to England by magic, to form an

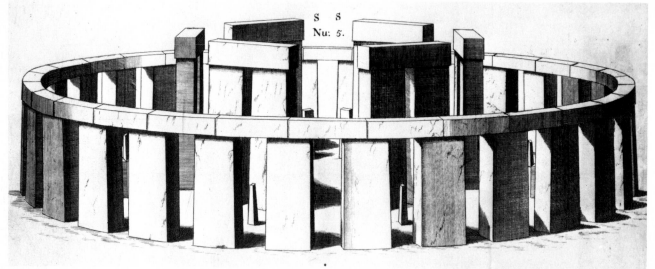

indestructible monument to the warriors of King Aurelius, uncle of Arthur.

From the 17th century, when Inigo Jones concluded that only the Romans could have built such a structure, successive generations of scholars have tried to solve the riddles of Stonehenge. There are still no answers; Stonehenge is just one of the 1,000 prehistoric stone circles found throughout Britain and northern France and archaeologists have found almost no clue as to their purpose. In fact the scarcity of finds supports the view that they were regarded as sacred places, kept clear of the usual debris of civilization.

Megalithic Engineering

Stonehenge seems to have been constructed in three phases, covering the period from 2200 BC to 1200 BC. It was a magnificent feat of megalithic engineering. The gigantic sarsen stones, great sandstone boulders arranged like doorways and capped with stone lintels, weigh up to 50 tons and were dragged to the site from the Marlborough Downs 30 km (20 miles) to the north, in a time when wheeled vehicles were unknown. The bluestones forming the smaller pillars came from the Prescelly Mountains in South West Wales, over 161 km (100 miles) away.

The 'how' of Stonehenge construction is intriguing enough but the important question is *why* the prehistoric builders should labour for centuries to build such an awe-inspiring monument.

Above: *A drawing of how Stonehenge might have appeared when it was first built.* ***Right:*** *Stonehenge as it appears today.*

The picture above shows a modern-day aerial photograph of Stonehenge. The arrangement of the stones indicates that Stonehenge was probably an astronomical observatory, built for astronomer-priests who would have used it to chart the movements of the celestial bodies.

As far back as the 18th century Stonehenge investigators realized that the stones of Stonehenge are aligned to the midsummer sunrise. From the centre of the circle, facing out through one of the massive arches to the ceremonial entrance, it is possible to see the sun rise directly over the great pillar known as the Heel Stone. Detailed analysis has shown a whole series of astronomical alignments which would explain why Stonehenge was built in this precise spot, regardless of the problems posed by bringing stones from distant quarries.

Many experts now believe that Stonehenge was an astronomical observatory, built under the instructions of astronomer-priests who used it to chart the movements of the celestial bodies and draw up a calendar for planting, harvesting and breeding cattle. If the sun and moon were regarded as gods, this would

explain the grandeur of a structure that could have served as a religious centre, a place of worship and ritual. Cremated human remains have been found at the site, which might indicate human sacrifice, or possibly the funeral rites of revered leaders.

If these theories are correct, then a remarkable level of skill and knowledge must have existed in prehistoric times, passed on by word of mouth from generation to generation, and eventually lost. Some people believe that the Druids, the priestly class of Celts in the late centuries BC, inherited some of the scientific knowledge of the megalithic priests. Caesar described them as astronomers and philosophers who refused to commit their learning to writing, preferring to pass it on by word of mouth. They were rumoured to have magical powers but earned a bad name with bloody rituals.

The Force of the Ley Centres

From the earliest times there has been a belief in the magical properties of the stones themselves and some modern investigators are convinced that all stone circle sites are linked by lines of force that carry a powerful psychic energy. The idea is rooted in the 1920s discovery by Alfred Watkins that prehistoric sites seemed to be linked in straight lines across the countryside. He called these lines 'leys' and decided that they were tracks used by prehistoric man, using the sites as landmarks. Since then the idea has grown up that leys are invisible lines of earth energy, felt by people who were more in tune with the rhythms of nature than modern man and marked by sacred sites. A spot like Stonehenge, where several leys converge, is like a powerhouse storing huge amounts of energy, energy that could have been harnessed by the builders to accomplish what seems to be an impossible task.

Remarkable numbers of UFO sightings have been reported at megalithic sites, especially Stonehenge, where filmmakers making a pictorial record of the stones in 1977 captured strange flying objects giving off brilliant lights, one hovering motionless over the site for 50 minutes. Some ley enthusiasts maintain that extra-terrestrial visitors are attracted by the elemental force of the ley centres.

Above: *Inigo Jones's reconstruction of Stonehenge in 1725.* **Left:** *A recent photo of Stonehenge showing two central pillars. Many believe that the stones themselves have magical properties and some modern investigators are convinced that all stone circle sites are linked by lines of force carrying a powerful psychic energy.*

Standing Stones

AND EARTH ENERGIES

The splendid megaliths, the prehistoric standing stones, circles and tombs of Europe, seem to have an eerie magic of their own, especially as they stand dark against the dawn sky or the red of the sunset.

Some are much larger than Stonehenge: at Carnac in Brittany, more than 2,600 stones stand in parallel lines, 10 stones or more abreast, stretching into the distance as far as the eye can see. At Avebury, just a few kilometres from Stonehenge, the circle covers 11.5 ha (28½ acres). Others stand alone, like deserted sentinels.

Astronomical Alignments

Investigators have pointed out astronomical alignments in many of them. One of the most spectacular is Long Meg and her Daughters in Cumbria. At midwinter the sun sets directly over Long Meg, a 2.8 m (9½ ft) high stone standing outside the circle.

Often megalithic builders seem to have carried their astronomical alignments outside the circles, positioning standing stones so that they lead the eye to a particular point on the horizon, where the sun or moon rises or sets at a significant point in its cycle.

Ley hunters have traced hundreds of other alignments connecting prehistoric sites such as standing stones, earthworks, tombs and ancient crosses.

At Boscawen-un, near Land's End in Cornwall, six standing stones, including one in the circle itself, run in a perfectly straight line for 5 km (3 miles). In the same area, rich in prehistoric monuments, another ley runs from Men-an-tol (the Stone of the Hole), for several miles

Above: Stones at Carnac, in Brittany, France. There are more than 2,600 such stones, standing in parallel lines.

Right: Long Meg standing alone outside a circle of stones in Little Salkeld in Cumbria.

through a single standing stone and a prehistoric village to Castle-an-Dinas, a hilltop enclosure thought to date from the Iron Age. The Arbor Low ley runs for 26 km (16¼ miles) from the ancient sacred well of St Bertram in Staffordshire through the circle-henge of Arbor Low, an iron age camp, the Hay Top tumulus and the round barrow of Top Low in Derbyshire.

The Megaliths' Ancient Powers

The early Christian Church was sufficiently worried about the power of the ancient stone sites to attempt to Christianize as many as possible, and churches often incorporated some of the stone into their walls. In the Middle Ages a religious ritual took place every 25 years at Avebury, when one of the stones was attacked as a symbol of the church's fight against evil.

Even in the 20th century, many prehistoric sites have been associated with pagan fertility rites or witchcraft ceremonies, presumably because the participants are convinced of their special power. Almost every circle or stone has its own set of legends. Many are sup-

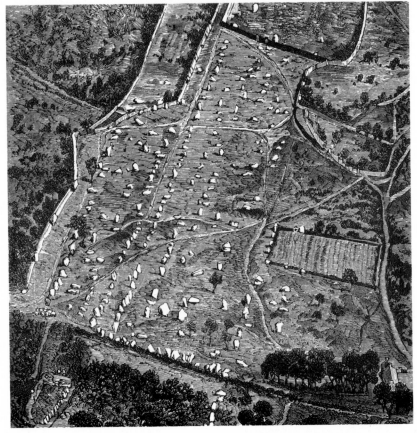

posed to have healing powers. At Men-an-tol, children suffering from bone diseases or consumption were passed three times through the hole in the stone, then dragged three times round the outside in an anti-clockwise direction. The cure was supposed to be just as effective for rickets or a crick in the neck. The Rollright Circle in Oxfordshire, a 30 m (100 ft) diameter circle known as the King's Men thought to date from 1500 BC, has a long-standing reputation for knitting broken bones.

Magnetic Strengths

Some modern investigators think that, instead of writing off the folklore and legends accumulated over the centuries as nothing but imagination, we should consider whether there is indeed some form of natural energy which has led to belief in their magical properties.

Professor John Taylor of King's Col-lege, London, in a series of experiments with a magnetometer, confirmed that there was more magnetic strength at the top of a megalith. The Dragon Project, a group of researchers led by Paul Devereux, set up a series of field experiments in 1978 at the Rollright Stones. Using electronic devices capable of detecting the minutest traces of all forms of energy, they registered changing energy readings around the time of the sunrise. The megaliths also registered slightly higher radiation levels than other historic sites, which might indicate that the megalith builders chose sites that were naturally radioactive, perhaps because they were rich in uranium.

Serious investigation of such possibilities is still in its infancy but it is possible that prehistoric man had an instinctive feel for natural sciences which has been lost with a more developed, urban lifestyle.

Top left: The outer ring of stones and ditch at Avebury.
Bottom left: Standing stones at Carnac, Brittany.
Below: Men-an-tol, Cornwall. It used to be believed that children who crawled through the hole would be cured of rickets.

The Earthdrawings of Nazca

MARKINGS IN THE PERUVIAN DESERT

At Nazca, in the parched desert plain of southern Peru, there is a vast tableau of strange markings, patterns and pictures. Some are very straight; some form geometric patterns; others make up enormous drawings of birds, fish or animals.

These are believed to date from somewhere between 400 BC and AD 900, though they took several centuries to complete. No one knows why they were made or who was meant to see them.

They were formed by removing a thin layer of dark stone to reveal the yellowish-white soil underneath. On the ground it is difficult to follow these lines at all; the form and extent of 'the world's largest work of art' can only be seen from the air.

A Guide to the Constellations?

The first researchers on the scene decided that the lines were astronomically aligned and the whole work was a giant guide to the movement of the constellations. Maria Reiche, a German mathematician who moved to Nazca in 1945, discovered that a number led straight to the point of sunrise or sunset at summer and winter solstices and that the points on the horizon mark the seasonal appearance of stars.

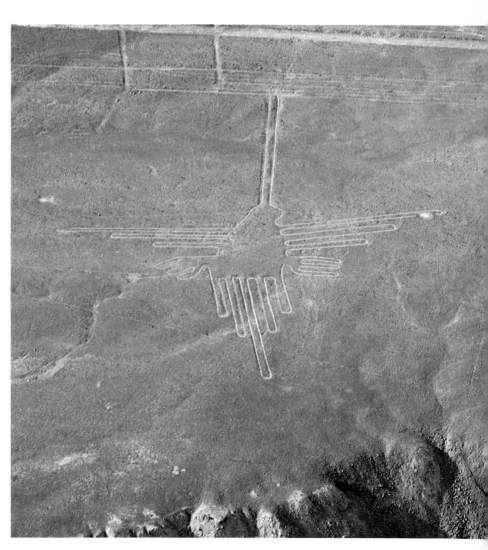

In 1968 astronomer Gerald Hawkins called this theory into question. He analysed the lines and their relationship with the heavenly bodies by computer but found no significant amount of matching. He decided their patterns were completely random.

Viewing from Above

Members of the International Explorers' Society set out to prove that the Nazca Indians could have viewed the patterns from the sky in balloons. Clues came from pictures that resembled balloons, kites and flying men on Nazca pottery and textiles and and from the 'burn-pits', circles containing blackened rocks, within the lines. Analysis showed that the rocks had been subject to intense heat, which could have come from a fire used to heat the air in a balloon.

Even so, the idea of high-flying Nazca Indians is only one of many possible answers and still leaves the big question: why would the ancient people of Nazca spend centuries drawing straight lines in the desert and flying over them in balloons?

***Opposite**: In the desert between the Ica and Nazca Valley in Peru a giant's picture-book of animals and birds, straight lines and geometrical figures was drawn on the ground many centuries ago. The figures can only be seen properly from about 600 feet up in the air. **Left**: Drawing of a spider. The lines were made by removing the stones which carpet the ground, to lay bare the whitish soil beneath. There are thousands of lines, some of them running straight with astonishing accuracy for miles. **Above**: This figure of a hummingbird is 100 yards (90 m) long.*

The cone of Glastonbury Tor rising out of the landscape with (inset) the Chalice Well.

Glastonbury
AND ITS LEGENDS

The enigmatic cone of Glastonbury Tor rises steeply out of the landscape to dominate the town, just as it dominated the swamplands of ancient times. The ruined church of St Michael stands on the top, the ruins of the great abbey below and a man-made path that winds seven times around the Tor may have been designed as a prayer route for early pilgrims.

Ley hunters show that a line drawn through the longest unbroken stretch of land in Britain, along the line of the May-day sunrise, runs right through Avebury and Glastonbury to St Michael's Mount in Cornwall. Along its length are many churches dedicated to St Michael – traditionally the leader of the angels in their fight against the forces of darkness – because they were built on the sites of pagan ritual.

The Holy Grail
Glastonbury was the earliest Christian centre in the British Isles but centuries before that the Tor was a sacred pagan site. Some of the most colourful and persistent holy legends have grown up around the area and the story goes that Joseph of Arimathea, the rich Jew who received Christ's body after the crucifixion, brought Christianity to Britain in AD 63, building the first church at Glastonbury and bringing with him the Holy Grail. In medieval legend, the Grail was the cup used at the Last Supper, the vessel holding the key to the ultimate meaning of life. To preserve the secret of the cup, Joseph was supposed to have buried it at the foot of the Tor. Today, it is often said to lie deep in the spring known as Chalice Well, where the waters have a reddish colour.

The legendary exploits of King Arthur and his knights of the Round Table are inextricably linked with the quest for the Holy Grail and Glastonbury's claim to be the last resting place of the holy vessel were boosted when excavations identified nearby Cadbury Castle, a massive prehistoric earthwork, as the most likely site of Camelot, Arthur's headquarters.

Another version of the beginnings of Christianity says that the first church at Glastonbury was built when Jesus himself came to Britain as a youth, accompanying Joseph, a tin trader who would have landed his cargo at St Michael's Mount – at the southern end of the ley line. There is, however, no historical evidence to suggest that the young Jesus ever came to Britain and the early Christian writings make no mention of Joseph when talking about Glastonbury. The Grail legends seem to have grown up in the 12th and 13th centuries.

The Thorn Bush and Zodiac
Another Glastonbury story, that a thorn bush in the abbey grounds is a direct descendant of the thorn that sprang up in full flower where Joseph's staff rested, seems to have been popularized by an 18th century innkeeper with an eye to increased trade.

The Glastonbury zodiac is a further example of the strange tales attached to the area. This is a giant zodiac circle said to be visible from the air, covering a 17 km (10 mile) radius, where features of the landscape – roads, hills, hedges and ditches – outline all the signs of the zodiac. It was discovered in the 1920s by Katherine Maltwood, who saw the legendary Round Table as the terrestrial zodiac and the quest for the Grail as the search for the meaning of life.

Whether or not the stories have any factual basis, there is undoubtedly a powerful magnetic attraction about the place, a pull that has drawn worshippers from the earliest times and still catches the imagination of modern visitors.

Secrets of the Maze

A COMPLEX LABYRINTH

The origins of the maze are lost in antiquity, their purpose magical, religious or symbolic according to their time in history.

The most renowned of all mazes was the home of the famous Minotaur at Knossos in Crete. The story was that the wife of King Minos of Crete fell in love with a bull and that the offspring of their union was the ferocious half man, half bull. Minos imprisoned him in a complex labyrinth and every year forced the city of Athens to sacrifice seven youths and seven maidens to the monster. Once inside the labyrinth the victims soon became hopelessly lost and were unable to escape. The Greek hero Theseus offered himself as one of the sacrificial victims and, with the help of the king's daughter, Ariadne, used a ball of thread to mark his way through the maze. Once the Minotaur was slain he was able to retrace his steps.

Archaeologists have found no trace of the Cretan maze and there is no firm evidence that it ever existed, but the idea of a labyrinth as a magical or religious symbol seems to have been used by many races from ancient times. It shows up on coins, rock carvings and mosaic floors, in the carvings on Indian temples, in the lines of Nazca in the desert of Peru, and in the Christian era on the floors of churches or carved on tombstone effigies.

Designing Mazes

There are two basic maze designs. The puzzle type has many different pathways, some leading nowhere, others ending up where they started, and is meant to baffle and confuse anyone trying to reach the centre. The other is a spiral, a single path winding back and forth, doubling back on itself so that finding the centre means following the entire pathway without ever crossing the same spot twice.

One explanation of the maze pattern is that it represents the conquest of death, so that to gain the centre and return again to the outside world is to achieve a symbolic conquest of death and experience rebirth. In many widely differing civilizations a spiral is used to represent the ever-repeating pattern of life: spring and autumn, sunrise and sunset, birth and death. Or perhaps the maze pattern represents a triumph over all that is worst in human nature, and that we have to slay it as Theseus slew the Minotaur.

Christian Symbolism

In Christian symbolism, the maze was used to represent the journey from birth to Heaven, with only one true pathway qualifying the believer for eternal life. Mazes were often laid out in the floor of medieval churches, like the famous 12 m (40 ft) example in Chartres cathedral in France. Another, at Amiens, destroyed in the 19th century and replaced by a copy, had the figures of the archbishop and the three architects inlaid in white marble.

These church mazes may have been used for a penance, with penitents following the pathway on their knees, reciting prayers at stations along the way. The centre of these mazes was known as Jerusalem and worshippers may also have trodden them as a symbolic pilgrimage.

Other churches, including Alkborough in Lincolnshire, Guildford St Mary in Surrey and Dalby in Yorkshire, had turf mazes laid out nearby. There are still a few examples of turf mazes to be seen in Britain, though many others, once cut in

A maze's purpose might originally have been magical, religious or symbolic, according to its time in history. Its origins are lost in history. Below is a diagram of the famous mazes at Versailles which were created in the 17th century at the time of Louis XIV.

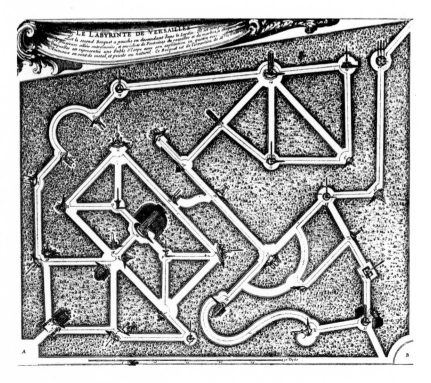

village greens or on commons, have disappeared. In their day they were used for dances and processions, all with a ritual element about them.

Intricate Networks

Turf mazes were often known as Troys or Troy Towns, supposedly because the walls of Troy were built as a labyrinth to confuse and trap the enemy, but this may have been a later invention to explain something whose origins have been forgotten over time.

In the 16th and 17th centuries, mazes were taken up by gardeners who designed intricate networks of pathways enclosed by hedges, like the famous Hampton Court maze, first planted in the reign of William III. These were purely for entertainment purposes, though they sometimes preserved a link with the past by incorporating a temple or a sculpture, lurking like the Minotaur in the centre of the maze.

Above: A maze cut in turf at Troy Farm, near Somerton, Oxfordshire. Old mazes are often called Troys or connected with places named Troy. In the old days they were used for dances, processions and games, all with an element of ritual in them.
Left: A circular maze has been inscribed on a tombstone at Alkborough in Humberside.

Landscape Figures

CARVINGS IN THE HILLSIDES

A map of Britain's ley lines shows that the mysterious White Horse of Uffington, created to gallop for ever across the Berkshire hillside, forms an isosceles triangle with the other horse carvings on hillsides at Pewsey and Cherhill in Wiltshire. Those who believe that leys mark tracks of electro-magnetic energy think these figures may form part of some sort of special power web.

The Uffington horse, a strange, stylized figure with spindly, disjointed legs, was mentioned in literature as long ago as the 12th century *Book of Wonders* but scholars have never managed to solve the secret of White Horse Hill; no one knows who carved the horse, or why, or when.

Some historians believe that it was cut in Saxon times, to celebrate the 9th century victory of Alfred the Great, ruler of Wessex, over the Danes. Others have shown that its abstract form bears a strong resemblance to horses depicted on Iron Age coins, several of which were found in the Uffington area and are now housed in museums. The horse may have been cut into the turf as early as 350 BC in honour of the goddess Epona, the guardian of horses.

It might have been used as a focus for the religious rituals which survived as the Uffington 'pastime', last celebrated in 1857. This was a festival linked to the

Above: *The White Horse of Uffington.*

144

Right: One of the most famous landmarks of the South Downs in Sussex is the Long Man of Wilmington. Below: The Cherhill White Horse, near Calne, Wiltshire.

periodic 'scouring', or cleaning, of the lines of the figure, when local people turned out in their hundreds. When the hard work was done, they celebrated the restoration of the horse.

There are no mysteries about the origins of the Pewsey and Cherhill horses. The Cherhill horse was created in 1780 by a doctor named Christopher Allsop who directed his labourers from a hill 1.6 km (1 mile) away, shouting instructions through a megaphone. George Marples cut the one at Pewsey in honour of the 1937 Coronation.

The thousands of years separating the cutting of the horses seems to weaken the theory that they are connected by a triangle of leys but it could be that their creators were impelled to choose those powerful spots by some form of energy in the atmosphere.

The Cerne Giant

The other great mystery figure of the English landscape, the Cerne Abbas giant in Dorset, lies directly on the line of the midsummer sunrise, extending from Stonehenge through the prehistoric settlement of Grovely Castle and ending at Puncknowle Beacon on the south coast.

The Giant, 55 m (180 ft) tall, brandishing a 37 m (120 ft) club, is often called 'the rude man of Cerne' because of his enormous erect phallus and could have been the symbol of an ancient fertility cult. As late as the 19th century locals believed that if a barren woman slept on the hillside, she would become fertile again. Even today, couples visit the Giant before a wedding if they want to make sure of having children, and girls who want to keep a boyfriend who is losing interest, or wives whose husbands are straying, walk right round the figure in the hope of reviving the relationship.

He may be as much as 1,500 years old, possibly representing a Celtic god called Nodens, though the giant was once known locally as Helis and in the 13th century Walter of Coventry spoke of the god Helith who was worshipped in the district. As there is no reference to the figure in historical documents before 1751, there are claims that he is far more modern. A local tradition says that he represents a corrupt churchman, Thomas Corton, and was cut after the dissolution of the monastery in 1539; yet another school of thought maintains that he is a 17th century folly.

Without further evidence, the Giant remains another of the world's strange landscape sculptures defying explanation.

Raining Frogs and Fish

ANIMALS FROM THE HEAVENS

Shoppers in Birmingham who were caught in a sudden, sharp rainstorm in 1954, found something heavier than raindrops showering down on them. Hundreds of tiny frogs fell from the sky, bounding off umbrellas and the shoulders of raincoats and hopping away across the pavement. It happened again in London in 1977, when small boys filled boxes full of frogs and men shook them from their hat brims.

Reports of creatures and other strange matter raining from the skies go back more than 2000 years. In AD 200 a Greek historian reported such a heavy fall of frogs that the inhabitants of one area had to brush aside heaps of them before they could walk along the street and the smell from the corpses was so great that towns had to be evacuated.

A Shower of Sprats

In England in 1666 a shower of sprats, whiting and smelts came from the sky

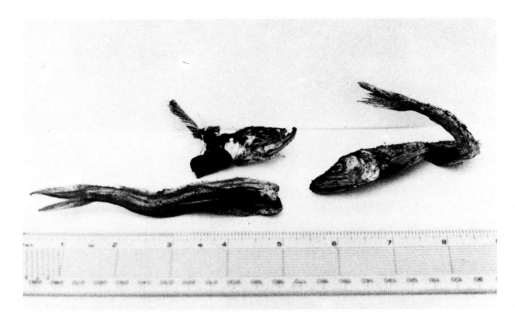

Left: A fish fall in East Ham in London, May 1984. *Far left*: 'Raining Cats, Dogs and Pitchforks', an ironic illustration of an unusual event by the famous 19th century artist, George Cruikshank. Frogs and fishes are among the most commonly reported falls. Thousands of small frogs rained on a house in Buckinghamshire in 1969 and thousands more fell in the desert in Morocco in 1977.

and the fish were sold for dinner in Dartford and Maidstone. A yellow cloud appearing over Paderborn in Germany in 1892 disgorged hundreds of mussels. In Wales in 1856 the astonished inhabitants of Mountain Ash, Glamorgan, saw two showers of live sticklebacks, 10 minutes apart. Some were taken to London Zoo in Regent's Park, where they were found to be normal and healthy. Thousands of snakes were found on the ground after storms in Memphis, Tennessee in 1877, crawling over one another in piles in an area confined to two city blocks. In England in 1911, heavy rain in Eton, Berkshire, left the ground covered with jelly, containing eggs of some species of insect, which soon hatched into larvae. Golfers in Bournemouth in 1948 found the course littered with herrings after a storm.

Baffling Showers

The usual down-to-earth explanation for the creature rains is that a whirlwind has sucked them up from one place and deposited them in another. However, a whirlwind would surely be a noticeable phenomenon and no whirlwind is normally reported in conjunction with the falls. Also, it would have to be a very selective whirlwind, picking up fish or frogs but no pondweed, leaves or other debris and often disgorging them in an orderly manner in one small area. Many fish falls last far longer than any whirlwind: in 1918, when hundreds of sand eels fell on a suburb of Sunderland, in England, a marine biologist reported that the fall lasted for a full 10 minutes.

A whirlwind is even less convincing as an explanation for the peculiar substance,

looking like thin flakes of meat, 5–7½ cm (2-3 in) square, that fell on Olympian Springs, Kentucky, in 1876. One analyst said that it was lung tissue.

An American journalist, Charles Fort, spent many years researching unexplained phenomena from obscure reports in newspapers and journals and his published works include enormous lists of strange rains: ants, worms, snails, lizards, toads, stones, manna, ice blocks.

Fort suggested, perhaps only half seriously, that the answer lay 'somewhere aloft', where gravity does not operate, in some planet or 'super-Sargasso Sea' which catches up things from earth, whether creatures or debris, and holds them until they are shaken down by a storm.

Without some equally unscientific theory, it is difficult to find an explanation for the shower of several hundred hazelnuts that fell in Bristol, in March 1977, in a street without nut trees. The nuts were ripe and ready for eating, though they would not normally be ready until autumn. Just as baffling was the rain of mustard and cress seeds, followed by showers of pea and bean seeds, that fell on three Southampton houses in 1979. The occupants called in the police but no explanation was found; they planted the seeds and they grew normally.

Some parapsychologists believe that these phenomena are linked to psychokinesis, where the power of the mind can moved objects and a disturbed person, usually an adolescent, can unconsciously cause disturbances. However, it is hard to accept that such a disturbance could produce living plants or creatures.

Lost Worlds

THE KINGDOM OF ATLANTIS

The Greek philosopher Plato, writing in the fourth century BC, described it as an idyllic place, rich in gold and silver, surrounded by lush vegetation, its people highly cultured and skilled in engineering and architecture. The name has gone down in history as an earthly paradise: the fabled kingdom of Atlantis.

Plato's Story

Plato's story came from account handed down by the famous Greek statesman Solon. He had heard from Egyptian priests of the powerful empire ruled from the island of Atlantis, where a once-virtuous people became corrupted by their life of luxury. When they tried to make war on Greece and Egypt, the all-powerful god Zeus meted out wholesale punishment and within 24 hours Atlantis was overtaken by volcanic eruption followed by a tidal wave and vanished for ever beneath the sea.

Aristotle, Plato's pupil, believed that Atlantis was an invention, moulded to fit Plato's political theories, but the idea of a lost paradise is so fascinating that the search for its location has continued ever since.

Plato's account dates the tragedy at about 9600 BC and places Atlantis 'beyond the pillars of Hercules', the modern Straits of Gibraltar, so that it would be somewhere in the Atlantic Ocean. Until recently, the most popular theory was that part of the long mountainous ridge running under the Atlantic from Iceland to Tristan da Cunha was once above water, before Ice Age glaciers melted and the seas rose, about 12,000 years ago. Twentieth-century geologists conclude that this is impossible: for thousands of years the Atlantic ridge has been rising rather than sinking.

Later Stories of Atlantis

When Christopher Columbus returned from his travels with tales of a new continent across the ocean many writers, including Sir Francis Bacon, identified Atlantis with America, though there was no level of early civilization in North America that could have given rise to such a legend.

In the first half of this century an American psychic, Edgar Cayce, claimed that he had mentally visited Atlantis while in a trance state. According to him, the inhabitants had already developed X-rays, television and anti-gravity devices. Before it sank in 10,000 BC, the inhabitants had fanned out to Egypt, the Pyrenees and South America.

He gave the site of Atlantis as Bimini, a small island in the Bahamas, forecasting that 'a portion of the temples may yet be discovered under the slime of ages of sea water ... expect it in '68 or '69.' Amazingly enough, in 1968 divers found two parallel lines of massive rectangular stones, which could have been a road or the walls of a harbour, off the coast of North Bimini.

Since then experts have disagreed over whether the stones are man-made or a natural phenomenon. In 1970 John Hall, Professor of Archaeology at Miami University, examined them and concluded that they were a Pleistocene beachrock erosion with no evidence of the work of a human hand. Then, a few years later, new expeditions found a masonry block with a sophisticated tongue-and-groove joint and, a few kilometres away, several marble columns.

Crete

Even if the Bimini road does mark the site of a lost city, only Cayce's strange prediction links it with Atlantis. The most widely accepted modern theory is that Plato might have been describing Bronze Age Crete, the most highly developed civilization of the ancient world, impressive in its art and architecture, ruled as a powerful kingdom, the fertility of the land ensured by a sophisticated irrigation system. The entire civilization collapsed suddenly at the height of its power in about 1500 BC, just about the time that the volcano of Thera, not far to the north, erupted disastrously. This version assumes that Crete was swamped by a tidal wave, giving rise to the story of a land disappearing beneath the sea.

This would mean that not only did Plato position Atlantis wrongly but also, perhaps because of misunderstandings in the original translation from the Egyptian, he was wildly wrong about the date of the tragedy. It would also mean that Atlantis has a place in history.

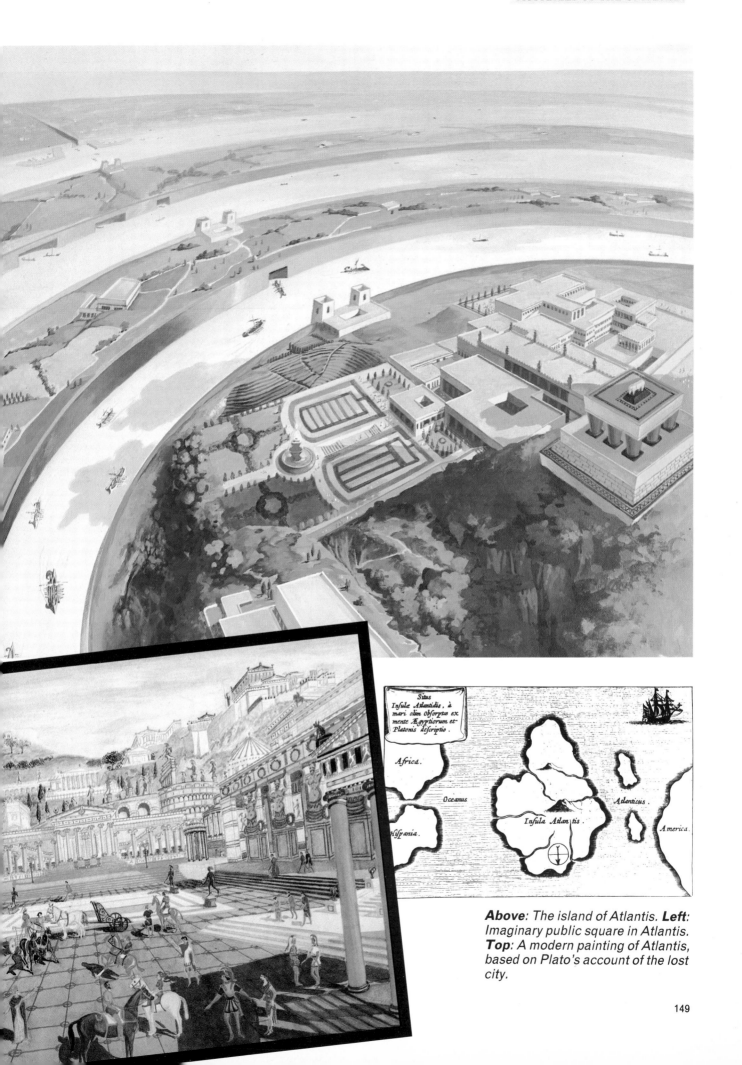

Above: The island of Atlantis. **Left**: Imaginary public square in Atlantis. **Top**: A modern painting of Atlantis, based on Plato's account of the lost city.

149

Above: 'Paradise Lost', by John M

Inset: A scene from the film 'Lost H

James Hilton.

The Garden of Eden

EARLY VISIONS OF PARADISE

The idea of a perfect place, a place of happiness and peace, which once existed on earth and might one day be rediscovered, is tantalizing and seductive. In the Middle Ages, people thought that the Garden of Eden still existed somewhere on earth, just beyond known horizons.

Over the centuries, there have been many accounts of lost worlds, which have been claimed to be the cradle of mankind, chief among them Lemuria and Mu. Both were vast continents; Lemuria once joined Africa and Malaysia and Mu, situated in the Pacific Ocean, was twice the size of Australia.

The Land of Lemuria

The name Lemuria was invented by the 19th-century zoologist Philip Sclater, when fossils of lemurs, ancient ancestors of the monkey, were discovered in both Madagascar and Malaysia. Sclater noted many other parallels between the plant and animal life of the two areas, even though they were separated by thousands of miles of sea. Some of the scientists of the time, excited by Charles Darwin's theory of evolution, seized on this as a way of explaining the lack of fossil remains of the evolutionary stages between apes and humans and decided that Lemuria was where man began.

The Lemurian story was widely publicized when a Russian psychic, Madame Blatavsky, claimed that aliens had taught her the secrets of the lost continent, where the inhabitants communicated only by psychic means. According to her, Lemuria sank beneath the waves millions of years ago but survivors escaped to Central Asia where their descendants evolved into today's Hindus.

The Lost Continent of Mu

In the mid-19th century historians trying to decipher the puzzling alphabet left by the vanished Mayan civilization in Central America decided that they had found references to a land called Mu, sunk in the sea after a great volcanic eruption 8,000 years before. The French archaeologist Augustus le Plongeon used the same system of interpreting the alphabet to read symbols on the walls of Mayan ruins and evolved a whole story of the life and loves of Mu's queen who escaped the catastrophe and fled to Egypt where, as the goddess Isis, she founded a new civilization.

Then Colonel James Churchward claimed that while serving with the British Army in India he learned the secret of Mu from Hindu priests. They taught him to read a forgotten language and, from tablets hidden in Indian temples, and corresponding tablets from Mexico, he managed to decipher the history of Mu, the original Garden of Eden. Man had evolved there and colonists had gone out to all corners of the earth to found the earliest civilizations before the country disappeared in a gigantic explosion 12,000 years ago.

In 1926 Churchward published his book *The Lost Continent of Mu* though he was never able to substantiate his story by producing the tablets, which had disappeared again after he had read them. Geologists have found no evidence of a sunken Pacific continent but his story found ready believers and his books continued in print until well into the 1960s.

The Longing for Paradise

There are strong oriental traditions of an earthly paradise, a place where the inhabitants have discovered the secret of defeating time and preserved a wisdom and knowledge that existed long before the dawn of modern civilization. James Hilton used the idea in his novel *Lost Horizon*, calling the place Shangri-la and setting it in the Himalayas but it is often known as *Shambhala*, meaning 'quietude', and could exist in the desolate regions of China or a hidden valley in the Tibetan mountains, untouched by outside influence.

Whether such a community really exists as a modern-day Eden or, as many holy men of the East maintain, it is a place of the spirit to be discovered only by spiritual comtemplation, the wish for such a place is yet more evidence of man's longing for a perfect refuge from all the ills of the world.

1825)
based on the book by

The Great Pyramid

THE PYRAMID OF GIZA

The Great Pyramid of Giza rises from a rocky plateau in majestic splendour, its very bulk awe-inspiring, challenging men to fathom its secrets.

There are 40 pyramids standing along the banks of the Nile but among them the Great Pyramid stands supreme. No picture can do justice to its immense size: it stands 137 metres (450 ft) high and covers 5.25 ha (13 acres) of ground, enough to take in Westminster Abbey, St Paul's Cathedral and the great cathedrals of Florence and Milan. Well over 2 million vast blocks of limestone, each weighing from 2 to 15 tons, went into the building – more stone than has been used by every church and cathedral ever built in England.

Geometric Precision

The pyramid was designed with geometric precision, its base a perfect square, its corners almost exact right angles, its sides accurately aligned with the four points of the compass.

It stands on a perfectly levelled site and is such a remarkable feat of engineering that many have supposed the pyramid was built by super-human builders – from refugees from Atlantis to visiting spacemen – but archaeologists now believe that the level foundation was created by building a mud wall around the plateau, flooding the area within, then smoothing away bumps revealed as the water gradually drained away. Stones were moved from quarries by means of sledges and rollers, though whether they were positioned by means of ramps, or by some type of lifting equipment, remains a puzzle.

A Tomb for King Khufu

The reason for the need to build such a structure is lost in time. Most modern Egyptologists accept the straightforward explanation that the pyramids were designed as tombs, built to protect the bodies of the pharaohs for ever more. The Egyptians believed that the soul could only live on if the body was preserved, so once the corpse was mummified it was important to seal it in a tomb that would be safe from intruders. The Great Pyramid was designed as the final resting place for the powerful and ruthless King Khufu, known to the Greeks as Cheops.

Unfortunately no bodies have been discovered in any of the pyramids. Stone coffins, or sarcophagi, have been found but they are invariably empty, often closed and apparently untouched. The bodies could have been stolen by grave robbers but thieves would have broken into the tombs to carry off the valuables buried with the pharaohs, not the corpses themselves. On the other hand, the pyramids might have proved such an obvious attraction for thieves that priests might have decided to remove the bodies and bury them secretly elsewhere.

No such simple explanation applies to the Great Pyramid, for when the King's Chamber was discovered the entrance corridor was completely sealed by three huge granite plugs and the only way to gain entry was by tunnelling laboriously round them. And though the King's Chamber had never been penetrated before it contained only an empty sarcophagus with its lid missing. It seems that after all the years of preparation the body of Khufu was never laid in the pyramid.

Why Was the Pyramid Built?

Over the past 200 years there has been endless speculation about the purpose of the pyramid, often so wild that it earned the name of 'pyramidiocy'.

Then author Peter Tomkins put forward the idea that the astronomer priests of Egypt used the money advanced by Khufu for a magnificent tomb to finance a monument to their own learning, deceiving him into thinking he would be buried there. With Dr Livio Strecchini, Professor of Ancient History at a New Jersey college, he worked out that the Great Pyramid served as an observatory, that it was a landmark from which the geography of the ancient world was worked out, that the builders knew the precise circumference of the earth and possibly the length of the earth's orbit around the sun, the acceleration of gravity and the speed of light.

Whether the pyramid is merely a marvel of engineering or proof of a vast body of knowledge, hidden for centuries, it is a perplexing place of wonder.

Pyramid Power

A VITAL FORCE OF NATURE

Through an intricate system of mathematical measurements, it was claimed the Great Pyramid had foretold major events, such as the exodus of the Jews from Egypt, the death of Christ on the cross and the beginning of the Second World War.

The Shape of the Pyramid

There have been many reports of the strange powers of the pyramid extending far beyond Egypt and the amazing building itself. The effects seem to centre on the pyramid shape, whether made from cardboard, metal or plastic.

Biologist Lyall Watson, author of *Supernature* suggested that the shape of the Great Pyramid might act as a focus for some form of energy.

Electrical Equipment

Other scientists have found that pyramids exert some strange influence over electrical equipment. In 1968 a team attempting to X-ray the pyramid of Chephren, a successor of Khufu, hoping to locate a hidden chamber that might contain a body, had to give up their project within 12 months. Their equipment went haywire within the vicinity of the pyramid, producing different X-ray pictures of the same area at different times and creating more puzzles than it solved.

Pyramid Power

Pyramid power caught on as a fashion in the 1960s, when pyramid shapes were tried out as solutions for medical and psychological problems. Sleeping under a pyramid tent was reputed to cure insomnia, calm hyperactive children, get rid of menstrual cramps or revive a flagging sex drive. In California there was even a craze for hat-sized pyramids, which were meant to recharge the brain.

There are many people who believe that a few minutes spent sitting under the shape of a pyramid to meditate, or simply resting and thinking, brings a peace and clarity that helps to lessen stress and renew energy.

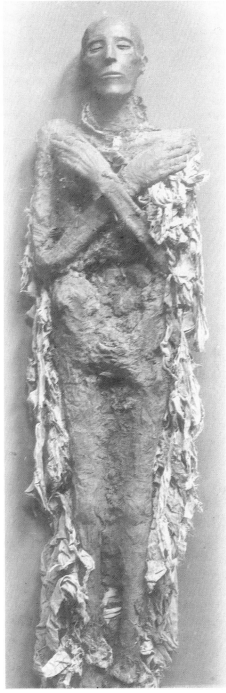

Above: The Egyptians went to enormous trouble and expense to preserve the bodies of the dead by mummifying them, so that the soul would live on. Modern experiments suggest that, for some unknown reason, the shape of the pyramid retards the decay of flesh and assists mummification.
Left: The Great Pyramid – passage from the second to the third gallery.
Far left: The Pyramid of Chefren at Giza.

CHAPTER SIX

THE
SPIRIT
WORLD

◆

There are many psychics who claim to be on friendly terms with the spirit world and there are many more people who have seen – or heard – a ghost. Spirits come in all guises, kindly or terrifying, sad or angry, bringing comforting messages or warnings of disaster.

The apparitions that haunt our stately homes, the battlefields of past centuries or the high seas are hard to investigate: they refuse to appear to order and seldom stay to answer questions. They may be ghosts of the dead, 'psychic photographs' projected into the present or even tricks of the mind but whatever the explanation they continue to fascinate generation after generation.

Left: 'The Spectre Monk', a photograph by the ghost-hunter and Picture Post *photographer Robert Thurston Hopkins.*

Ghosts

THE HISTORY OF HAUNTINGS

Ghosts, those spirits of the dead that rise to haunt the living, have fascinated every civilization from the dawn of time. They appear on the clay tablets of the early Babylonians, the wooden engravings of the Middle Ages and the oil paintings of the 17th and 18th centuries.

Ghostly Legends

Spirit legends have deep roots in many cultures. The Chinese have more than 20 different kinds of ghosts but the two main types are the *shen*, the good spirits, and the evil, *kuei*. Japanese ghosts take many hideous forms, but one, which sometimes takes the form of a fox and sometimes a beautiful woman clad in white, flowing robes, is supposed to bewitch anyone who looks on her.

The ancient Greeks and Romans were convinced that apparitions frequently interfered in the lives of men. Brutus was haunted, first by the accusing ghost of Caesar whose assassination he had plotted, then by an apparition that appeared when he was planning his strategy for

battle against Anthony and Octavian. Brutus was alone in his tent when a spirit 'horrifying in its gigantic proportions and pale, emaciated face' appeared. 'I am your evil spirit,' it announced. 'You will see me again at Philippi.' It appeared again the night before Brutus died on the battlefield of Philippi.

Ghosts and Christianity

Biblical references to ghosts include the spirit of Samuel, raised by the witch of Endor to warn King Saul of the forthcoming defeat by the Philistines and Job's nerve-wracking account. His description was a familiar account: 'Fear came upon me, and trembling, which made all my bones to shake. Then a spirit passed before my face; the hair of my flesh stood up.'

The early Christian church had no difficulty in accepting the reality of ghosts and Evodius, a friend of St Augustine, met several of them: 'I remember well that Profuturus, Privatus and Servitius, whom I had known in the monas-

tery here, appeared to me and talked to me after their decease and what they told me happened.'

Ghosts were sometimes seen by the church fathers as the harbingers of temptation. St Anthony, who believed in the hardships of the flesh as a way of attaining godliness, was plagued by phantoms, including a ghostly woman of great beauty who tried to tempt him into the sins of the flesh.

Every European country has its own famous ghosts. Pope John XXII, in 1323, was so impressed by reports of the ghost of Avignon, where a French merchant haunted the town as a punishment for sins of adultery committed there, that he sent a Benedictine prior to investigate. On 14 May 1641, the ghost of Cardinal Wolsey appeared at the bedside of the Archbishop of Canterbury to warn him of bad times ahead if the people did not turn back quickly to God. In 1721 the well-known German scholar Professor Schupart was attacked by a poltergeist as his friends looked on. In modern times there have been reports of haunted theatres, lighthouses, motorways, airfields and even council houses.

Space–Time and the Past

Researchers tend to believe that certain events or people from the past may have left an imprint on a locality because of the strong emotions experienced there, like an echo lasting for years or even centuries. This explains why ghosts are so

often associated with sites where there has been a lot of misery, violence or murder.

Another theory is that the whole of the past is recorded somewhere in space–time, just as though it was on film. Normally we perceive only current events as they are recorded, but occasionally a momentary time-warp allows us a quick glimpse of the past, as though part of the film is being re-run.

Hauntings are familiar in all cultures throughout the world, even though the form of each apparition may be strikingly original. There may be both good and evil spirits. In modern times some researchers believe that certain events or people from the past may have left an imprint on a locality because of the strong emotions experienced there.
Above*: A ghost cat on a hearth rug.* ***Left****: Phantom priests of the Basilica of Le Bois Chêne in Domrèmy, France. The photograph was taken by Lady Palmer.* ***Far left****: An alleged photograph of the spirit of Lord Combermere at Combermere Hall, taken by Sybell Corbet on 5 December 1891, just at the time when Lord Combermere was being burnt alive.*

Spectral Armies

GHOSTLY BATTLES OF THE PAST

Reports of spectral armies reliving historic battles date back for centuries. Ghostly warriors have been seen at the site of the Scottish Battle of Culloden, fought in 1746, and headless war-horses gallop through a Wiltshire valley near Woodmanton.

In 1951 two English tourists holidaying in France watched a ghostly re-run of the Dieppe raid of 19 August, 1942. In the USA a number of people have reported seeing the Battle of Shiloh, where 20,000 soldiers died in the American Civil War, fought again by spectral troops.

The Battle of Edgehill

Britain's most famous phantom battleground is Edgehill in Warwickshire, where a bloody battle of the Civil War was fought between Cavalier and Roundhead armies in 1642. More than 40,000 soldiers were involved in the fighting, when Prince Rupert led the King's troops against the forces of Oliver Cromwell. By the end of the day the field of battle was strewn with the bodies of the dead and dying.

A few weeks later local people said that they had seen and heard the battle being fought again – and again. They saw the soldiers firing muskets and cannon, heard the clash of steel and the tumult of fighting, as well as the cries of the wounded. As the news spread, people from all the surrounding villages turned out, amazed as the armies 'appeared in the same tumultuous warlike manner, fighting with as much spite and spleen as formerly'.

King Charles I sent four officers to investigate the puzzling rumours of ghostly battles. They saw the fighting themselves and even recognized some of their dead comrades from the original battle, among them the Royalist standard-bearer, Sir Edmund Verney.

There have been many reports of ghostly battles being fought over and over again. The picture above shows Maccabees' vision of the 'Army in the Sky'.

Below: The Battle of Edgehill fought between Cavalier and Roundhead armies in 1642. It is Britain's most famous phantom battleground. **Left**: The bowmen of Mons.

Visions and Portents

WARNINGS FOR THE FUTURE

Lord Thomas Lyttleton, an 18th-century womanizer, was woken on the night of 24 November 1779 by what sounded like the wings of a trapped bird. At the foot of his bed he saw the ghost of a girl he had seduced and deserted and whose despair had driven her to suicide. She pointed to the clock on the mantle, telling him that he had only three more days, to the exact minute, to live.

Next day he put a brave face on the story when he told his friends but as the time grew nearer, his fear grew. To cure his nerves, his friends set every clock in the house one hour ahead, so that the predicted hour of death came and went without incident. A much-relieved Lyttleton went to bed an hour later but, as the church clock struck the appointed time, he suddenly clutched his side and fell dead before the eyes of his horrified servant, William Stukey.

The Harbingers of Doom

Ghosts are often harbingers of doom, bringing dire warnings for the living or timing their appearances to herald disaster. In times of national crisis Abraham Lincoln is said to roam the corridors of the White House, while the ghost of a Regency politician haunts No. 10 Downing Street.

The ghost of the 17th-century Earl of Strafford returned more than once in an effort to avert a coming disaster: he appeared to Archbishop Laud, telling him of the bloody spectacle his severed head would make when 'on London Bridge 'tis raised' then in 1645 he appeared to King Charles I while he was staying at the Wheatsheaf Hotel, Daventry. He warned the King that he would suffer defeat if he confronted the Parliamentary troops camped nearby. The King's supporters forced Charles to ignore the warning and his army was crushed at the Battle of Naseby.

Part of the tradition of haunting is that anyone who sees his own wraith is about to die. The much-quoted example is the poet Shelley who was about to board a boat to cross the Bay of Spezia in Italy when he saw before him his own wraith. He died shortly afterwards, when the boat was hit by a sudden storm.

Apparitions as Life Savers

Not all the warnings conveyed by apparitions are ignored; sometimes they have saved lives. Britain's ambassador to Paris in the 1880s, Lord Dufferin, had a strange experience while staying with friends in Ireland. Looking out of his bedroom window one evening, he saw below a hunched figure, carrying what looked like a coffin. When the man looked up he had a clear view of an ugly, grizzled face, before both man and coffin vanished. No one in the house could explain what he had seen.

Several years later Dufferin, attending an official function in the Grand Hotel, Paris, was about to step into the lift when the operator looked up – and he saw the same grizzled face. Shaken, he stepped back and let the lift go. That second's hesitation was to save his life, for when the lift reached the fifth floor the cable snapped and it plummeted down to the bottom, killing all the passengers.

*There have been many instances of ghosts suddenly appearing to warn of impending disasters. **Far left**: Lord Thomas Lyttleton was well known in the 18th century as a womanizer. Here he is visited by the ghost of one of the many women he had seduced, warning him of his impending death. **Below**: Many strange events occurred during the First World War. Pictured here is a happening which was much talked about at the time: a vision of Jesus appearing as 'The Comrade in White'.*

An Adventure at Versailles

GHOSTS OF A SUMMER AFTERNOON

Versailles, near Paris in France, has been the scene of a number of accounts of ghostly visitations. None, however, has been more spectacular or unexpected than that which occurred on a summer afternoon in 1901. Two English women, Eleanor Jourdain and Ann Moberly, both eminently respectable scholarly women, were visiting Versailles. At the same time both suddenly experienced feelings of depression, loneliness, stillness and oppressiveness, and a 'heavy dreaminess' as though they were sleepwalking. They saw a number of people dressed in 18th century costumes, and concluded that they had seen ghosts. They published a detailed account of what they had seen in a book entitled An Adventure. **Far right**: *An 18th century illustration of Versailles with (inset) photographs of Eleanor Jourdain and Ann Moberly.*

On a summer afternoon in 1901 two English women, Miss Ann Moberly, the head of an Oxford women's college, and Miss Eleanor Jourdain, a school headmistress, visited Versailles and found themselves experiencing something that has since become a major ghost story of the century.

Adventures in the Past

After touring the palace they went to look for the Petit Trianon, where Marie Antoinette, surrounded by her courtiers, used to amuse herself by pretending to be a peasant woman or a shepherdess. They found it surprisingly difficult to locate and as they walked, the afternoon seemed suddenly still and oppressive. Then they saw a number of people in 18th-century costume, among them two men in grey-green coats and three-cornered hats and a man in a heavy black cloak, his face heavily disfigured by the marks of smallpox.

Later, Miss Jourdain described 'the heavy dreaminess' of the atmosphere, which made her feel as though she was walking in her sleep, and the overwhelming feeling of depression and loneliness they had both experienced while watching the figures.

It was a week before they could bring themselves to discuss it with one another but when they compared notes they came to the conclusion that they had seen ghosts. Miss Jourdain was astonished to find that she had seen far more than her friend, including the figure of a fair-haired woman in a pink dress and a shady straw hat. Later she discovered that there had been several past reports that the ghost of Marie Antionette had been seen in the garden in a pink dress and a wide-brimmed summer hat.

When they returned to Versailles in 1904 they could no longer find the path that they had taken on their first visit, or the various landmarks they had seen along the way. It was only when they studied a map drawn in 1780 that they managed to identify the features of the garden that they both remembered seeing that August afternoon, including a cottage, a grotto, and a bridge over an artificial ravine, all features that had long since disappeared.

When their research was completed they published a detailed account of what they had seen, called simply *An Adventure*.

In the 1970s Dr Joan Evans tried to explain away the strange happenings, saying that what the two visitors had seen had to be Comte Robert de Montesquiou and his friends in costume, performing one of the 18th-century charades they were known to enjoy. However, this does not explain how the women had seen several features of the grounds that had been there in the time of Marie Antoinette but were no longer there in 1901; in fact, later investigators pointed out that the Comte de Montesquiou had moved back from Versailles to Paris several years before the 'adventure' had taken place.

Montesquiou would certainly not have been there in 1938 when a woman visitor walking near the Trianon saw a couple in 18th-century peasant costume pulling a small cart full of logs, who passed her without a sound and vanished into thin air as she turned to watch.

In 1949 an English family from Westmoreland saw a woman in a crinoline and a large picture hat, with long dark ringlets. She looked as solid and real as any of them and they assumed she was an actress, making some sort of film, until she disappeared before their eyes.

There have been several similar sightings at Versailles, all by people who have never heard of Miss Moberly or Miss Jourdain and their adventure, so it seems very likely that spirits from the past return to haunt Versailles.

The Flying Dutchman
A PHANTOM SHIP AND CREW

The original Dutchman was a sea captain, Hendrik van der Decken, who had been sailing from Holland to the East Indies when he ran into a fierce storm. He defied the Almighty to sink him and sailed on, ignoring all the pleas from his crew. For his blasphemy he was condemned to sail the seas for ever with a phantom crew.

A Royal Witness
Many sailors have told of sighting the vessel and of the bad luck that inevitably follows but the most eminent witness was Prince George, later to become King George V. He was sailing as a young Royal Navy midshipman on the *HMS Inconstant* off the coast of Australia in 1881 when, on 11 July, he recorded in the ship's log:

'At 4 am *The Flying Dutchman* crossed our bows. She emitted a strange phosphorescent light as of a phantom ship all aglow, in the midst of which the masts, spars and sails of a brig 200 yards distant stood out in strong relief as she came up on the port bow, where the officer watch from the bridge saw her, as did the quarter-deck midshipman, who was sent forward at once to the forecastle, but on arriving there no vestige nor sign whatever of any material ship was to be seen either near or right away to the horizon, the night being clear and the sea calm.'

Thirteen of the crew of *HMS Inconstant* saw the ghostly vessel and bad fortune quickly followed: the seaman who had first sighted her fell dead and news came of the death of the Admiral of the Fleet.

One of the most interesting sightings of *The Flying Dutchman* came from dry land. In March 1939 the 100 or so people sitting on the beach at False Bay, south-east of Cape Town, watched in amazement as a fully rigged sailing ship passed across the bay, its sails full though there was no wind that day. One moment it was there, the next it had vanished. Short of a mass hallucination, it is difficult to believe that so many people could have been mistaken in what they saw.

Haunted Houses

APPARITIONS THROUGH THE AGES

Royal homes, where history is made and so many dramatic and tragic events have occurred over the centuries, seem to harbour many spirits from the past and are a specially rich scene for ghost hunters.

The Ghosts of Glamis Castle

Glamis Castle, the turreted Scottish fortress in the Vale of Strathmore, is the Scottish home of the Queen Mother's family. Princess Margaret was born there, the first child in direct succession to the throne to be born in Scotland for 300 years.

The history of the Lyon family has not always been happy. In the 16th century John, the 6th Lord of Glamis, married Janet Douglas, whose family had earned the undying hatred of King James V. After Janet was widowed, he had her arrested on a false charge of witchcraft and plotting against the person of the king. She was burned at the stake in 1537 and her sad ghost still walks the Clock Tower of the castle.

There is also the story of a fateful game of cards played by a 15th-century Earl of

Left: *An imposing view of Glamis castle with its many turrets.* **Below:** *The ruins of Inshock, another Scottish haunted castle.*

Strathmore, a notorious drinker and gambler, and Lord Crawford, a huge, bearded man known as 'Lord Beardie'. The stakes were high, each man was determined to win and though a servant reminded them that the Sabbath was approaching, they refused to stop, challenging the devil himself to join the game. At midnight the devil appeared to tell them that, as their game was so dear to them, they could continue playing until the day of judgement.

Even now the doomed card players are sometimes heard in the night, arguing and swearing, and sleepers have woken to find the huge figure of Lord Beardie towering over them or seen him sitting brooding by the fireside.

The most persistent of the legends of Glamis concerns a 'monster', a first-born son born as a hideously misshapen beast, locked away in a secret room and living an unnaturally long life. Rumours spread through Victorian society from guests who had stayed in the castle and heard strange howls and snarls or saw a strange, shambling shape wandering through the corridors. In 1865 a workman who discovered a secret passage emerged white and shaking with terror over what he found there. Soon afterwards the man was hurried off to Australia with his whole family, their passage paid by the Earl of Strathmore.

There have been suggestions that the fearsome secret, said to be known only to the head of the family and passed on to his heir on his 21st birthday, concerned this monster – perhaps that its offspring still lived in some hidden room in the crypt or that its ghost visited some curse on each generation of the family.

There was certainly a secret and it must have been terrifying, for the 13th Earl was quoted as saying 'If you could only guess the nature of the secret, you would go down on your knees and thank God it was not yours.' Friends reported that, from the moment he heard the secret, he was a changed man, moody and morose. The 14th Earl was so horrified, when his turn came to hear the story, that he refused to pass it on to his son, so the ancient mystery of the castle still lies hidden.

The Wives of Henry VIII

Hampton Court, built by Cardinal Wolsey and presented to Henry VIII in an attempt to ingratiate himself with the King when he fell from favour, still preserves echoes of the turbulent events of Henry's marriages.

Catherine Howard, Henry's fifth wife, is the palace's noisiest ghost, frequently seen and heard running and screaming along the long gallery to the door of the Chapel Royal, her long hair flowing loose. When her adulterous affair with a handsome young courtier was discovered, the King refused to see her or hear her explanations. Convinced that if she could only talk to him face to face she could save herself from the scaffold, she made one last desperate attempt, breaking free from her guards and running down the gallery to beat on the door of the chapel, where Henry was attending a service, screaming for his attention. The King ignored her, the guards dragged her away and on 13 February, 1542, she was beheaded. Her ghost frequently repeats that one last attempt to save herself.

Anne Boleyn

Anne Boleyn, Henry's second wife, who was beheaded in 1536, has been seen several times, wandering miserably along the corridors, identified by the blue dress she wears in one of the Hampton Court portraits. Jane Seymour, the gentle, quiet girl who died in the house a few days after giving Henry the son he so badly wanted, sometimes emerges from the Queen's apartments, dressed in white and carrying a lighted candle as she walks along the Silver Stick Gallery and down the stairs.

After Jane's death, the baby prince was fostered by a nurse, Mistress Sibell Penn, who was to die of smallpox in 1568. She was buried at St Mary's Church, Hampton, but when the church was rebuilt in the early 19th century her tomb was moved and soon after that came reports of a thin, hooded figure in a grey robe – identified from the effigy on Mistress Penn's tomb – occasionally seen to walk through solid walls. A family living in the nurse's rooms in the palace were disturbed by whirrings and mutterings and eventually a sealed room was discovered containing an old spinning wheel, on which Mistress Penn may have spun thread for the baby prince's clothes.

Three former monarchs still visit Windsor Castle in Berkshire. Queen Elizabeth I has been seen in the library, also a favourite spot for King Charles I, who lost his head in the Civil War in 1649. Henry VIII was seen as recently as 1977, walking the battlements and disappearing into the wall.

Herne the Hunter

The most famous of Windsor's ghosts is Herne the Hunter who gallops through the park with his band of ghostly huntsmen and his pack of hounds in full cry. Herne was one of Richard II's huntsmen who hanged himself from a great oak on one of the forest rides when he was dismissed from his post.

In 1976 a young Coldstream Guardsman was found unconscious in the Great Park, collapsing from fright after seeing an apparition standing before him, dressed in hunting clothes and with a pair of stag's antlers jutting from his head. The description of Herne was unmistakable; according to tradition he was once saved from death by a magician who bound a pair of antlers to his head.

Herne has been seen many times over the centuries; before the oak was cut down in 1863 a number of visitors were shocked by the grisly sight of a dead man hanging from the branches. Queen Victoria used some of the logs from the tree for her own fire 'to help kill the ghost' but Richard II's forester has never left the castle grounds.

Hampton Court, in London, has been visited by many ghosts. **Far left:** *The ghost of Jane Seymour at Hampton Court Palace. Jane was the third of Henry VIII's six wives and died one week after giving birth to the King's long-awaited son. Her ghost is sometimes to be seen emerging from the Queen's apartments.* **Far left:** *(below): The Clock Court at Hampton Court Palace.* **Below:** *A magnificent illustration of Herne the Hunter, an apparition said to haunt the grounds of the Great Park at Windsor. Herne is supposed to gallop through the park with his band of ghostly huntsmen and pack of hounds in full cry, wearing a pair of stag's antlers.*

Borley Rectory

Many private houses also have their resident ghosts, and inexplicable happenings at Borley Rectory, on the Essex-Suffolk border, earned it the title of 'the most haunted house in England'. Borley, a gloomy mansion built in 1863, was home to the Reverend Henry Bull and later his son Harry, who lived there until 1927. Over the years there was an endless stream of strange happenings: bells rang and voices answered, there were unexplained footsteps and tappings in the night, a phantom coach and horses drove through the grounds, and several people saw a shadowy nun walking in the garden.

In 1929 psychic investigator Harry Price and his team were called in by the new rector, hoping to dispose of the haunted house rumours once and for all. The researchers heard bells and knocking, saw objects fly through the air of their own accord and experienced sudden sharp drops in temperature.

Price was so fascinated that he devoted years to studying the house and, from the scraps of evidence he pieced together, he decided that the disturbances were caused by the spirit of a 14th century nun, murdered after an illicit love affair.

Since then, other investigators have accused Price and some of the residents of the house of fabrication, but reports of strange happenings continued long after Borley Rectory was burned down in 1939. Passersby still heard thundering hooves, wartime air-raid wardens were often summoned to investigate lights at the ruined windows and cameras and electrical equipment failed mysteriously at the site. In 1943 excavations in the cellar uncovered a woman's skull.

A photograph taken at Borley seems to show a brick suspended in mid-air but an even more extraordinary photo was taken at Raynham Hall in Norfolk. A professional photographer was commissioned to take some pictures of the hall and he was setting up his equipment to take some shots of the magnificent staircase when he saw the ghostly figure of a veiled woman coming down the stairs. The resulting photo, pronounced genuine by a number of experts, shows the misty outline of a human figure.

Below: Borley Rectory, 'the most haunted house in England', built in 1863 and burnt down in 1939. Many strange happenings occurred there, even after the mansion was gutted.
Far right: A ghostly woman coming down the stairs at Raynham Hall in Norfolk, said to be Dorothy Walpole and photographed by Captain Provand in 1936.

Screaming Skulls and Other Apparitions

At Longleat, in Wiltshire, the ghost of a woman walks backwards and forwards along a passage at the top of the house, obviously in an agony of terror and grief. She is said to be Lady Louisa Carteret, who died in 1736. Her husband, Lord Weymouth, caught her with a lover and the two men fought with swords, up and down the passage where she now walks. Lord Weymouth is supposed to have killed the young man and buried him secretly in the cellar. The story was given substance when the remains of a young man in 18th century clothes were found under the cellar floor earlier this century.

Several old English houses have 'screaming skulls', so attached to their homes that they wreak havoc on anyone who attempts to move them. The skull at Bettiscombe Manor, a handsome 17th-century house near Sherborne, in Dorset, is said to belong to a black slave. The owner of the house, Azariah Pinney, was exiled to the West Indies in 1685 for his part in the Monmouth rebellion but he prospered there and in due course his rich grandson, John Frederick Pinney, returned to Bettiscombe bringing the slave with him. He is supposed to have promised the slave that he would return his body to his homeland in Africa after his death. However, Pinney died first and the slave was buried in the local church-yard. Immediately after his burial, bad luck affected the whole village and a constant moaning and crying was heard from the graveyard. Eventually the body was exhumed and the skull carried back to the house. The family tradition holds that anyone who removes it will die within the year. There is a story that one tenant, in the early 20th century, tried to get rid of it by throwing it in the pond. The next morning, it was back on the doorstep, waiting to be readmitted.

Another 'screaming skull' is now built into the fabric of the house it refused to leave, at Burton Agnes Hall in Humber-side. It belonged to Anne, youngest daughter of Sir Henry Griffith, who built the house at the end of the 16th century. Anne, who was devoted to her beautiful home, was murdered by robbers but as she lay dying she made her family prom-ise to keep her head in the house for ever. They did not keep their promise but from the moment Anne was buried, the house shook with a great banging and crashing and they were forced to do as she had asked.

Below: Bettiscombe Manor House, allegedly haunted. Right: The Tower of London, the scene of many alleged appearances of ghosts.

The Ghosts in the Tower of London

The building with the greatest number of unhappy ghosts is probably the Tower of London, which has seen many bloody deaths in its long history.

The earliest recorded haunting was in 1241, when 'a certain priest, a wise and holy man', saw St Thomas à Becket, murdered in Canterbury Cathedral 71 years before. Becket had been Constable of the Tower and apparently returned to prevent the building of some new walls. The priest saw the apparition strike a wall with his cross and demolish it.

Anne Boleyn appears more often in the Tower than at Hampton Court, for it was here that she spent the night before her execution on 19 May, 1536. Many sentries have seen her and, on occasion, after their challenges have been ignored, have run a bayonet through her, only to find themselves stabbing the air. One guard, seeing a light in the Chapel of St Peter ad Vincular where Anne was buried, looked through the window to see her leading a procession of courtiers and ladies in Tudor dress, all vanishing as they reached the altar.

Two other ladies beheaded at the tower seem to find it hard to leave the scene. Seventeen-year-old Lady Jane Grey was imprisoned there after her nine-day-rule and watched the execution of her young husband, knowing that she was to die later the same day. More than once, guards have seen her on the battlements on the anniversary of her death.

Margaret, Countess of Salisbury was 70 when she was condemned to death in 1541 but, as she was innocent of any crime, she refused to put her head on the block. She was chased round the scaffold by an axe-wielding executioner, who needed three strokes to sever her head from her neck and her ghost re-enacts this grisly scene at the execution site.

The path along the battlements between the Martin and Constable Towers has been nicknamed Northumberland's Walk because the ghost of a former Duke of Northumberland has been seen there so frequently, and the warders have also seen Sir Walter Raleigh, imprisoned for many years before his execution, in the Bloody Tower where his rooms were sited and on the battlements where he took exercise.

The saddest of all the many ghosts are the two little boys in white nightgowns, thought to be the two princes, Edward and Richard, murdered in 1483, who wander the Bloody Tower hand in hand, lost and bewildered.

Spiritualism

THE FOX SISTERS

When strange raps and knocks were heard at night in the small wooden-frame house in Hydesville, New York State, where John Fox and his family lived in the mid-19th century, no one dreamed that this would be a major landmark in the history of ghosts and mark the beginning of the spiritualist movement.

The rappings went on night after night, in March 1848, until Fox and his wife, devout Methodists, were convinced that they were being plagued by a restless spirit. Their children, 10-year-old Margaret and seven-year-old Kate, once they had recovered from their initial fright tried to make it into a game and imitated the raps. They found that the ghost seemed to answer them, as though it was trying to communicate.

Their parents listened in amazement to the raps. They decided to try to give the spirit the chance to 'talk' by calling out letters of the alphabet, so that it would rap whenever its chosen letter came round, to complete whole words and sentences.

Painstakingly, it spelled out its name, Charles Rosma, and explained that it was the ghost of a pedlar who had been murdered in the house and buried beneath the floor of the cellar. The story soon spread and, when a search party dug up the cellar floor, the remains of a man were found.

The Power of the Children

Hundreds of eager sightseers flocked to the house to hear the rappings for themselves, asking questions and receiving answers from the spirit. The Fox family could stand it no longer; they moved away, but found that the rapping moved with them. It was only then that they realized that the phenomenon was associated with their young daughters.

Soon the girls were in great demand to give demonstrations of their powers and many new and different kinds of manifestations began: they gave messages under hypnosis, furniture moved on its own, tables levitated, instruments were played by invisible hands. Several panels of investigators put the Fox sisters through a series of tests without being able to prove them guilty of fraud. One group reported that even when the children stood on cushions with both hands and feet tied, rappings came from the walls of the room.

The idea of communicating with spirits came as a tremendous boost to those whose belief had been shaken by Darwin's theory of evolution and Spiri-tualism, as the new religion was called, attracted converts by the thousand. 'Table-tapping' became all the rage.

Both girls married; however, both husbands died within a few years. Margaret turned to drink and gave demonstrations only when she had to, to earn a meagre living, but Kate went on attracting international attention. She was investigated in Britain by the eminent scientist Sir William Crookes, who was deeply impressed by her abilities.

A Confession of Fraud

In October 1888, Margaret stood before a packed audience in New York and confessed that her whole career was based on fraud. Kate did not contradict her and their opponents saw it as the end of the whole spiritualist movement. However, Margaret's attempt to demonstrate how the fraud had been committed was far less impressive than the phenomena witnessed by so many people over the years and shortly afterwards the sisters announced that they had been offered a large amount of money if they would confess to cheating. They were in serious financial difficulties at the time and this was the reason for the false confession.

The controversy that had followed them all their adult lives intensified. Though many believers still supported them, they were never again able to regain their standing and both died penniless in 1895. But the movement their story had started went on from strength to strength, spreading all over the world.

The Fox sisters lived with their parents in Hydeville, New York State in the middle of the 19th century. It was when Margaret was ten and Kate seven that strange rappings were heard in the night in the small wooden framed house. Only later was it realized that the rappings were those of a ghost and that the phenomenon was connected with the two sisters. Thus was the spiritualist movement born. **Far left:** *An engraving of the Fox sisters levitating a table at Rochester.* **Inset:** *Margaret Fox.* **Below:** *Kate Fox.*

Doris Stokes

A MODERN MEDIUM

Doris Stokes, who died in 1987, was probably the most famous medium of the 20th century. Her approach was always matter-of-fact. There were no darkened rooms or strange manifestations; she described herself to be like a telephone exchange, putting spirits in touch with the loved ones they had left behind.

She was *clairaudient*, which means that she heard rather than saw spirits, but she would be warned by a blue light flickering over the heads of her audience when a message was coming through. She chatted in a matter-of-fact way with the spirits, telling them to speak up or to wait their turn. She said that the spirits would often tell her off when she failed to understand quickly enough, saying 'Get on with it woman!' Occasionally, when several spirits were trying to talk at once, she would stop and tell her audience: 'I'm making a pig's ear, don't believe a word I'm saying.'

A Natural in the Modern World

She was born Doris Sutton, the daughter of a blacksmith in Grantham, Lincolnshire. Her extraordinary psychic ability showed itself quite early on but she did her best to suppress it. 'I really didn't want to know. I wanted to be normal and ordinary.' As a young WRAF, in the early days of the Second World War, she went with friends to the 'spook show' at the local Spiritualist church and one medium after another told her: 'One day you'll be doing this.'

She never trained as a medium but started passing on messages to people who crowded into her home, then gradually earned a reputation on the spiritualist circuit.

Doris Stokes received thousands of messages for others over the years but none was more welcome than the message she heard from her dead father, after her husband John had been reported missing in action during the war. A medium at the local Spiritualist church told her that he was dead but when she arrived home her father came to tell her that 'John is not with us', and that she would have proof of what he said on Christmas Day. After that, though she heard officially from the War Office that John was dead, she knew this was a mistake – and, on Christmas Day, the news came that he was alive.

It was her brilliantly successful American tour in 1978 which made her a household name. Letters began pouring in from all over the world, her books became best sellers and she was in demand for prime time television shows. In Australia she filled the Sydney Opera House; when she was billed for the first time at Britain's London Palladium the tickets were sold out within an hour and a half.

Different Sorts of Messages

Many sceptics were convinced by the quantity of personal information Doris Stokes managed to produce, details trivial in themselves but impossible for any outsider to know or guess. Sometimes, however, the message became confused. When she was sitting with the parents of Jayne MacDonald, one of the victims of the Yorkshire Ripper, the name Sutcliffe came through. Mrs MacDonald said that it was an old family name, so it was forgotten until the killer, Peter Sutcliffe, was finally arrested.

Doris Stokes chatted with many famous spirits, including the author George Orwell, pop stars John Lennon and Marc Bolan and her old friend Diana Dors. The conversations were sometimes serious, sometimes comic: after her 13th operation for cancer, the spirit of Dick Emery told her that the spirit world wanted her so much they were taking her bit by bit.

Perhaps her greatest achievement was convincing a great many people that they had nothing to fear from death.

Doris Stokes heard, rather than saw, spirits. She passed on messages to the living from their loved ones who had died.

Automatic Writing

THE LIVING AS TOOLS FOR GHOSTS

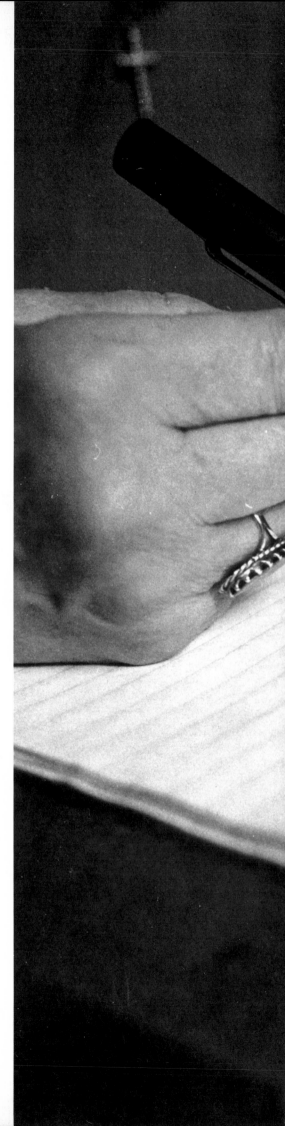

The argument over whether 'automatic writing' results from contact with spirits or simply from a different level of consciousness is likely to continue indefinitely. What is certain is some people have produced letters, literary works or musical compositions showing a level of skill and knowledge that the writers themselves do not possess – at least not on any conscious level.

Pearl Curran and Patience Worth

Pearl Curran was an ordinary American housewife who left school at 15 with little knowledge of history and no interest in literature but she became a prolific writer of poetry and prose full of accurate historical detail and the authentic language of the period she was writing about.

She claimed no credit for herself; she was only a tool for passing on the work of an English Quaker girl, Patience Worth, who died in 1641. Patience's life had been unsatisfying and she now longed to fulfil herself as a writer. She went on to produce thousands of poems and six published books as well as a great deal of other material.

Telka, the story of a girl living in Anglo-Saxon Britain, was a success in its own right but caused a furore in academic circles because the great majority of the vocabular used belonged to the Anglo-Saxon period, a feat difficult even for an expert scholar. *A Sorry Tale* was set in Palestine at the time of Jesus, telling the story of one of the thieves crucified with him and another, *Hope Trueblood*, was a story of Victorian England. In both cases, scholars found that the vocabulary and atmosphere of the books matched her settings exactly.

Patience delivered her material with remarkable speed, so that one evening Mrs Curran recorded 22 poems at one sitting. The style was literary and polished and Mrs Curran admitted that, a few years before, she would not have been able to understand her own books.

Rosemary Brown

Rosemary Brown, from south London, had no formal musical training and could manage only a few simple tunes until one day in 1964 she saw the composer Liszt standing beside her old second-hand piano. Suddenly he took over her hands and she was playing beautiful music with consummate ease.

After that many composers dictated their unpublished works, teaching her how to notate piano and orchestral works. She took down piano sonatas from Chopin, string quartets from Brahms and part of a symphony from Beethoven. She met and talked to all the composers and came to regard them as friends, each with his own personality: she found Chopin a perfect gentleman, Brahms strong and patient, Bach clear and methodical.

Experts who have listened to the works are divided: some are impressed and bewildered, admitting that it would take years of training to come up with imitations as good as Rosemary Brown's; others dismiss them as the work of a naturally gifted musician.

Matthew Manning

When Matthew Manning, who later became a famous healer, was plagued by a poltergeist as a teenager, he managed to channel his psychic energy into automatic writing and a man called Robert Webbe, who had once lived in Manning's house and died in 1733, communicated with him in this way for several years. Manning also found that he could produce sketches in the style of famous artists, completing them in a couple of minutes though they were of such a high standard they looked like originals.

Grace Rosher receiving 'spirit writing' through a pen propped up on her finger. **Inset**: *Manuscript of a D-flat Mazurka, received from Chopin by Rosemary Brown.*

Materializations

VISITATIONS FROM THE VOID

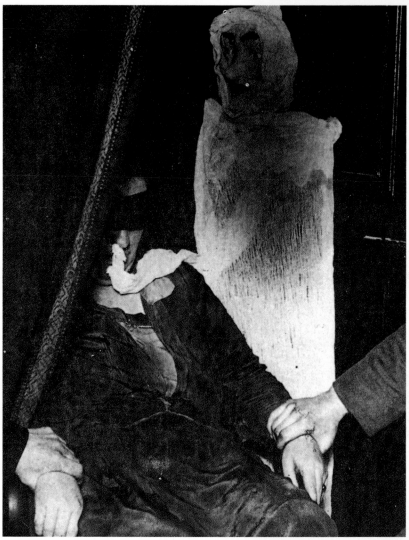

Modern mediums usually adopt a quiet, low key approach to the spirit world but in Victorian times more flamboyant methods were popular, with mediums apparently vying with one another to find a more impressive way of 'proving' the existence of their spirit contacts.

Materializations often began like luminous cloud which would generally form into a human hand, face or a complete form. The South American medium, Carlos Mirabelli, could produce the life-like forms of spirits known to his sitters, dressed as they would have dressed in life, able to answer questions and touch their loved ones. He gave demonstrations in full daylight, in test conditions and before eminent witnesses who were forced to admit that no trickery was involved.

Fraudulent Manifestations

Not all results were so impressive and investigations were often to prove that the mediums were no more than clever magicians. In the 1930s and 1940s Helen Duncan, from Scotland, was twice convicted of fraud when her sitters grabbed at an apparent materialization, only to finds themselves holding a handful of muslin. Mina Crandon, famous under the name of 'Margery' in the 1930s , was a Boston medium who produced thumbprints in wax, said to belong to her dead brother Walter. In fact they belonged to a living dentist who had once demonstrated the technique of obtaining prints in wax.

The Schneiders

Scientists all over Europe were keen to test Willi and Rudi Schneider, two German brothers whose gifts revealed themselves while they were very young, and most believed them genuine. At the age of 14 Willi was giving seances where he produced ectoplasm: one of the observers described it as a cobweb-like material which wrapped itself round Willi's face, then disappeared completely. At the same time a faint phosphorescent glow emitted from Willi's head, encircled it like a hat and was then drawn back into his body through his nose. At a later seance, when Willi was in a deep trance,

Olga, his spirit guide, materialized and danced for the assembled company.

Over the next five years more than 90 scientists, doctors, lecturers and other researchers took part in a systematic series of experiments with Willi and the long list of manifestations they witnessed included materializations of hands, arms and heads, loud knocking and sudden gusts of cold air.

By the time Willi was 20 his powers had declined markedly but by then his younger brother Rudi was giving seances

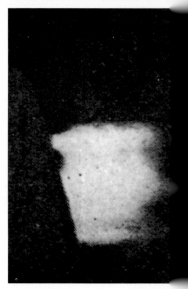

Franek Kluski, 'king of the mediums', demonstrating his extraordinary ability to produce concrete evidence for the existence of spirits from another space and time.

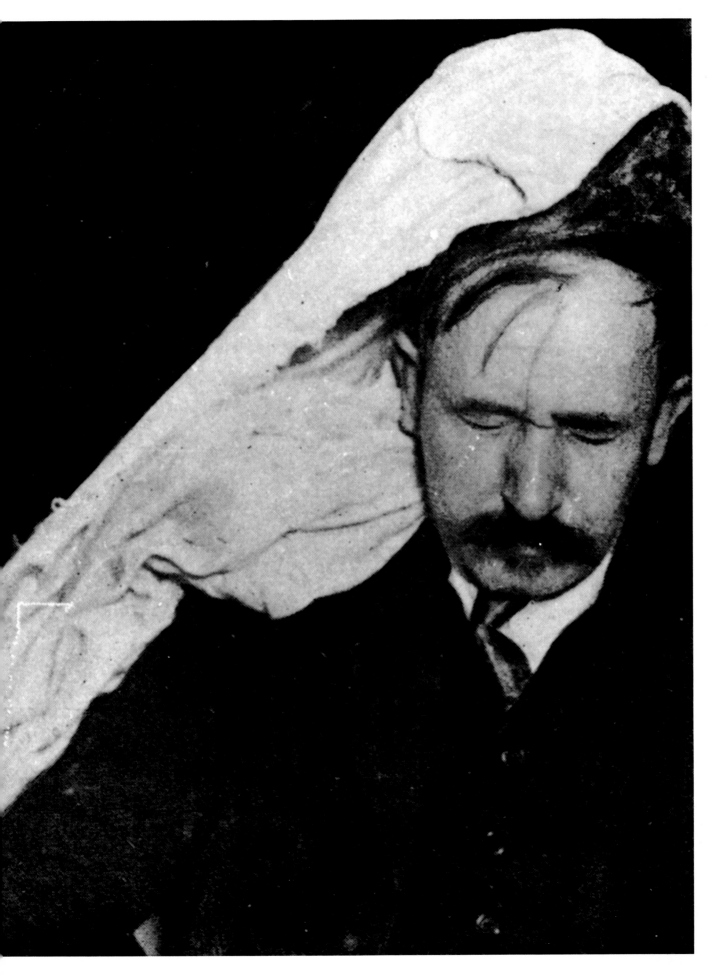

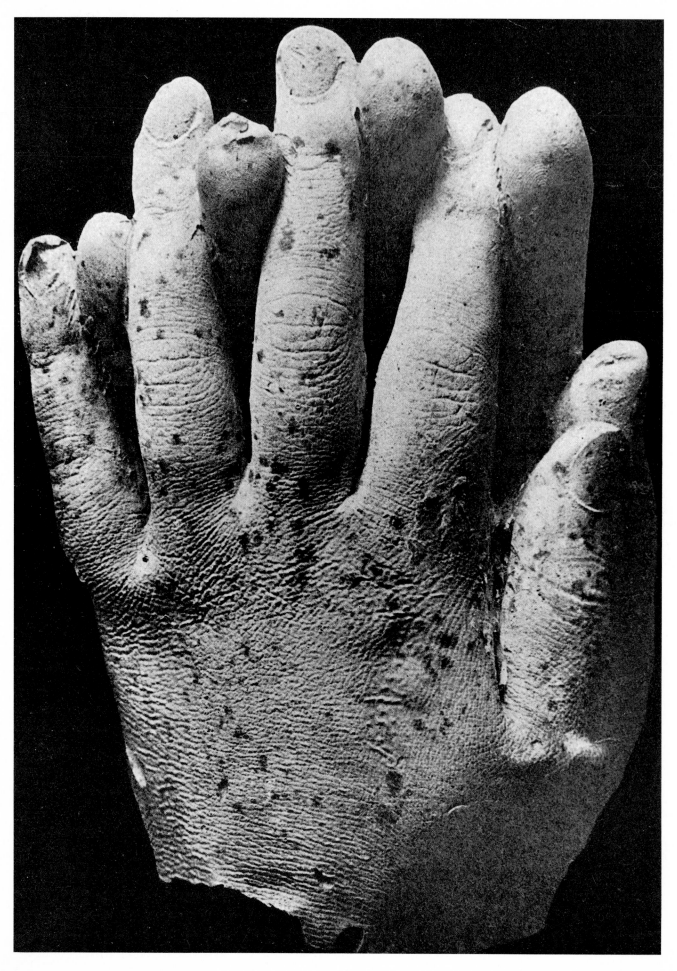

with the same spirit guide. After one seance the boys' father recorded: 'At yesterday's sitting there were at least thirty appearances of an almost six foot high phantom. At one time there were two such phantoms. One of them touched a member of the circle.'

Dr Eugene Osty, director of the respected French Institut Metaphysique, devised a 15-month investigation programme, installing infra-red photographic apparatus that could function in darkness and would reveal any physical interference from the medium. The physicist was impressed when the experiments indicated a powerful force coming from the medium and affecting the infra-red rays. Even at a seance under the strictest conditions, after Rudi had been thoroughly searched and locked in a room with every door, window and even keyholes sealed, a large apparition materialized.

Franek Kluski

Polish medium Franek Kluski was called the King of the Mediums by Dr Gustav Geley, director of the Institute Metapsychique Internationale de Paris because no one was able to explain away the extra-ordinary evidence he provided in his seances. He evolved the extraordinary technique of making wax casts of the faces and hands of the spirits by materializing the spirit's hand or face in a bowl of hot wax, then plunging it into cold water, leaving a wax 'glove' or the imprint of a face. These were later filled with plaster of Paris to make permanent moulds.

His seances were conducted in semi-darkness but investigators who held his hands all the way through could hear the spirit splashing in the bowl of water.

Between 1919 and 1923, Franek Kluski produced amazing animal manifestations, well-attested by witnesses of high repute. Professor F. W. Pawlowski of the University of Michigan described a dog with glowing eyes, a small animal resembling a weasel that 'ran over the table and smelt the hands of faces of the sitters with a small, cold nose' and a hawk-like bird that 'flew round, beating its wings against the walls and ceilings'. Professor Pawlowski was convinced that the bird could not have been smuggled into the room or out again by normal means as it vanished as suddenly as it had appeared.

Franek Kluski made wax casts of the faces and hands of spirits by materializing them in bowls of hot wax and then plunging these immediately into cold water, leaving impressions which were later filled with plaster of Paris to make permanent moulds. **Far left:** *Wax gloves (formed by hands materializing and leaving impressions in wax) made in the presence of Franek Kluski in Warsaw in 1921.* **Below:** *Kluski in Warsaw on 30 August 1919 with a bird materialization.*

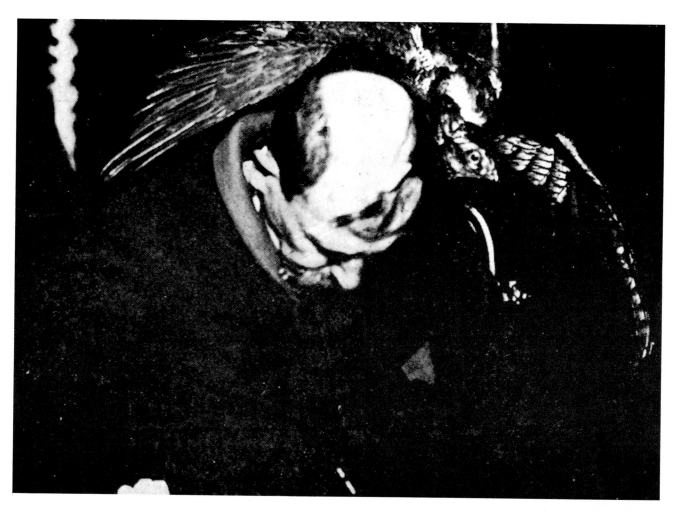

Poltergeists

DISTURBERS OF THE PEACE

Poltergeists are the noisy spirits that crash, bang and knock, move furniture, throw crockery and generally cause disturbance.

The word comes from the German and one of the earliest cases was recorded in Germany, at Bingen on the Rhein in AD 355. The citizens found themselves pulled from their beds by unseen hands, stones flew around and the whole village echoed with unexplained thumping and banging.

Since then, poltergeist disturbances have been reported all over the world. The 'greislie Gaist of Gye' became famous throughout Europe in the 14th century when a village in France was beset with strange noises and showers of stones, the people pushed this way and that by strange forces. Even a papal inquiry was unable to produce any explanation. In Italy in 1890 a leading psychiatrist, Professor Cesare Lombroso, saw bottles of wine smashed and shoes fly through the air unaided while he was investigating a poltergeist at a small inn near Turin.

Drumming without a Drummer

In England, one of the earliest well-attested poltergeist cases appeared at Tedworth in Wiltshire, beginning in the spring of 1662. It started after a one-time regimental drummer, a Mr Drury, was brought before the magistrate, John Mompesson, charged with obtaining money by false pretences. The magistrate let him off with a caution but confiscated his drum and ordered him to leave the district. Straight afterwards, drumming sounds filled Mompesson's house and a witness saw the drum rise in the air, all by itself, giving out loud booming sounds.

After several sleepless nights, Mompesson had the drum destroyed but the sounds continued. All sorts of other strange things happened: shoes were tossed about, servants were lifted aloft in their beds then set down again gently and Mompesson reported that 'in our presence and sight the chairs did walk about'.

Above: The Runcorn poltergeist of Cheshire in 1952 moved furniture around. Here, John Glynn surveys his wrecked bedroom in the afflicted house. *Right*: The case of a poltergeist in South Bromley, London – fertilizer fell from the ceiling in a garden centre and formed this face. The features changed several times and were recorded.

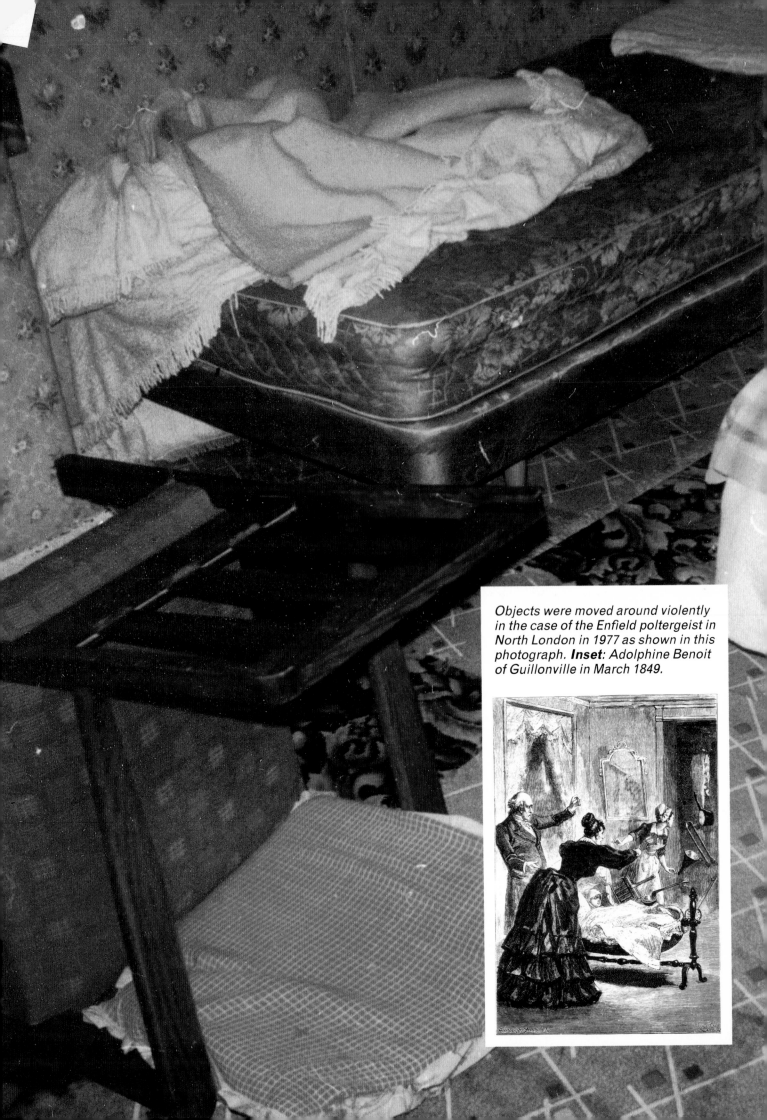

Objects were moved around violently in the case of the Enfield poltergeist in North London in 1977 as shown in this photograph. **Inset**: Adolphine Benoit of Guillonville in March 1849.

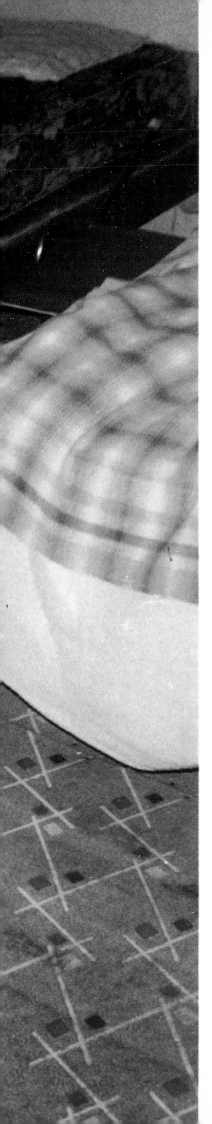

Among those who gave eye-witness accounts was the Reverend Joseph Glanville, chaplain to Charles II and a Fellow of the Royal Society. the disturbances continued for exactly a year and no explanation was ever found. The theory that Dury had returned to take revenge was soon disproved; he had been arrested for theft in Gloucester and sentenced to transportation.

20th-Century Disturbances

Poltergeists seem to be just as active and troublesome in the 20th century. Psychic investigators, journalists and police all witnessed strange phenomena in a rented house in Enfield, north London, the home of Mrs Peggy Hodgson and her four children. The Hodgson's nightmare began in September 1977 when 11-year-old Janet heard shuffling steps in her bedroom followed by knocking. A heavy chest of drawers moved by itself and other objects began to move unaided. Much more frightening was the effect on the teenage girls when deep, old men's voices came from them, though their lips did not move.

The poltergeist became terrifyingly violent: a heavy iron gate flew across nine-year-old Billy's room, narrowly missing him as he lay in bed and Janet was hurled into the air as she lay sleeping. Once a curtain wrapped itself round Janet's neck with such force that her mother had to fight to pull it off.

Researchers were unable to write off the phenomena as childish pranks. Specialists from Pye Electronics who visited the house were amazed to find that even though their video equipment was in full working order it would not function inside the house. A policewoman, who was called to the house several times by the terrified family, described seeing a chair lift into the air, move sideways and then float back to its original position. Psychic researcher Maurice Grosse tried to communicate with poltergeist using a method of knocks but the conversation ended when a cardboard box filled with cushions leaped at him from the floor.

Janet's sister, Margaret, provided some clue about what was happening when she began crying in her sleep: 'Go away you ten little things.' While still asleep, she gave details of people, including a baby, three girls, two boys and an elderly couple, one of whom she identified as Frank Watson, 'the man who died in the chair downstairs.' The distrubances lasted for three years before they ceased as suddenly and mysteriously as they had begun.

There have a number of careful and well-documented investigations of poltergeist activities and many parapsychologists feel that they 'focus' on a young person in the household, that there is some sort of psychic energy released at the time of puberty that can create disturbances and move physical objects, as a form of involuntary psychokinesis or mind over matter.

The Coffins That Would Not Stay Still

However, there are plenty of cases which cannot be explained by any theory so far put forward. For instance, the sacrlege perpetrated at Oistin's Bay on the island of Barbados, where the Chase family had buried thier two daughters in a stone-builtd tomb which already contained the wooden coffin of Mrs Thomasina Goddard. In 1812, when the children's father, Thomas, died and the tomb was opened to receive his coffin, mourners were shocked to find the girls' lead caskets upended against the wall, though Mrs Goddard's coffin stood in its usual place.

Eight men carried the lead coffin of Thomas Chase into the tomb and replaced the other coffins in their original positions. Stonemasons then cemented into position the marble slab sealing the tomb. But when it was opened again four years later for the funeral of a boy relative, the lead coffins were once more standing on end against the wall. Once again, the caskets were replaced. The walls of the tomb were thoroughly checked for any other means of entry and resaled, but the same thing happened at a funeral two months later and again in 1819.

The governor of the island, Lord Combermere, intervened , supervising the orderly arrangement of the three larger coffins in a straight line, the three smaller ones on top of them, with fine sand sprinkled aroud them. When the entrances slab was cemented into place, he fixed his seal to one of the jams. The following year, having checked that his seal was intact, he had the tomb opened only to find that the Chase family caskets were scattered all over the tomb. There were no masks in the sand and, as always, only Mrs Goddard's coffin was untouched.

The family, dreading further notoriety, had their relatives buried in the nearby Christ Church cemetery, leaving the tomb – and presumably its poltergeist – silent and abandoned.

ACKNOWLEDGEMENTS

Half title page: Topham Picture Library

Jacket: Robin Scagell/Science Photo Library

Aerofilms 132, 144 *left*

Associated Press 55

Barnabys Picture Library 130–1, 136 *top*, 144, 145

BBC Hulton Picture Library 18, 20–1, 31, 40, 64–5, 66–7, 75, 86, 87, 149 *below right*, 160–1, 162

Janet and Colin Bord 133 *below*, 140–1, 143, 170 *below*

Aldus Archive 6, 10, 36, 37, 38, 39, 46 *left*, 48, 54–5, 58, 98 *top*, 130, 148–9, 180–1

Camera Press 8–9, 22, 28, 32–3, 50–1, 67 *inset*, 68–9

Colorific! 12, 14, 32, 34–5

Robert Estall 134, 137

Mary Evans Picture Library 19, 23, 25 *inset*, 26, 44–5, 56, 59, 60 *left*, 62–3, 78 *top*, 82, 94, 97, 99, 104, 105, 110, 112 *below*, 113, 125, 126 *top*, 126–7, 128–9, 133 *top*, 136 *below*, 142, 148–9 *below*, 154–5, 158, 159 *below*, 160, 161 *inset*, 163, 166, 167, 170 *top*, 171, 172, 173, 174, 176, 177, 181 *inset*, 182, 182–3, 185, 186–7, 188–9

Fortean Picture Library 13 *below*, 26–7, 42–3, 42 *top*, 44, 57, 60–1, 88, 96, 98 *below*, 100, 101, 103, 108, 109, 115, 118, 119 *top*, 127 *top*, 128 *inset*, 134–5, 140 *inset*, 147, 184, 186

John R. Freeman and Co. Ltd/The Fotomass Index 84, 150–1

John Frost Historical Newspaper Archive 30–1, 73 right, 74, 82–3

Giraudon 165

Robert Harding 46–7

Michael Holford/British Museum, London 146–7

Images Colour Library 13 *top*, 159 *top*, 168, 169

The Keystone Collection 63 *inset*

Kobal Collection 21, 90–1, 110–1, 114, 150 *inset*

Dr. Jean Lorre/Science Photo Library 122–3

Mansell Collection 78 *below*, 80, 81, 155

Tony Morrison 138–9, 139 *right*

Popperfoto 16, 52–3, 70, 72–3, 76, 77, 92, 93, 102, 106, 107, 116, 117, 129 *right*

DATE DUE			